A JOHN CATT
PUBLICA...

FERGAL ROCHE

MINING FOR GOLD

STORIES OF EFFECTIVE TEACHERS

First Published 2017

by John Catt Educational Limited
12 Deben Mill Business Centre, Old Maltings Approach,
Melton, Woodbridge IP12 1BL

Tel: +44 (0) 1394 389850 Fax: +44 (0) 1394 386893
Email: enquiries@johncatt.com
Website: www.johncatt.com

ISBN: 978 1 911382 44 7

Set and designed by John Catt Educational Limited.

Praise for
Mining for Gold

'This book is distilled inspiration, a brilliantly easy-to-read reminder of how great teachers have an influence way beyond their knowledge. In illuminating the impact of the teachers of those who influenced him, Fergal Roche serves up an uplifting demonstration of the way teaching is a craft, a vocation, a role driven by moral purpose, and a hugely undervalued set of skills. This is a book to enthuse and inspire. It's a testament to the intoxicating power of great teachers, to the way they do something so complex while making it all seem so apparently effortless.'

Geoff Barton, General Secretary, Association
of School and College Leaders

'This is a book unlike any other I have read. It's not a book that draws on anything other than his rich experience of teaching and teachers. It is an honest and powerful reminder to us all about the joys, challenges and power of our wonderful profession. Uplifting, honest and funny, I was swept along from one chapter to the next. For those moments when what you need is an entertaining read, this is the book for you!'

Andy Buck, Managing Director #honk, Founding
Director, Leadership Matters

'What comes over more than anything for me is the everlasting impact of the work of good teachers on the whole person development of learners. The passion of the teachers for their subject is also strongly felt and readily enthuses learners: indeed, liking a teacher and the enjoyment of a subject are inextricably intertwined.'

Dr Jane Jones, Senior Lecturer & Subject Director of
MFL Teacher Education, King's College, London

'This is a thoroughly engaging book. Heads are often asked the question "What makes a great teacher?" We all have different opinions in response to that enquiry but Fergal Roche has skilfully distilled the essence of great teaching in this book through his own personal experiences. I thoroughly recommend it to all school leaders, teachers and those thinking of entering the teaching profession.'

Dr Jon Cox, Headmaster, The Royal Grammar School, Guildford

'This is a book for all teachers, whether they are just embarking on their first placement or have been in the profession for years. It is also for senior managers and for those who have responsibility for shaping our educational establishments. Reflecting on personal and professional experiences at all stages of his career, Fergal ingeniously weaves together insights which illuminate the highly complex and skilled role of the inspirational teacher. He causes us to question anew the essence of what teaching and learning really is and the particularly individual qualities which not only make a teacher unique, but more importantly really effective. The focus on teacher well-being, support and respect for the profession is very timely, as we seek to attract and retain high-quality and inspirational individuals who truly make a difference to the world in which we live. This is an inspirational and uplifting read, but with many challenging and often sobering messages which all of us who work in education should take note of.'

Sally Eales, Senior Lecturer,
BEd Primary Education Programmes Leader,
University of St Mark & St John, Plymouth

'This is an amusing, inspiring and thought-provoking collection of stories and reflections. Fergal's unwavering belief in the power and importance of teachers serves as a basis for all of us to consider what we do to enable, or conversely, inhibit, them from doing an amazing job. A refreshing contribution to the educational debate.'

Liz Robinson, co-headteacher, Surrey Square Primary School
Chair of Governors, International Academy of Greenwich

Contents

To my wife, Heather, and my children,
Camilla, Marcus and Nina, who are still trying to teach me

Foreword

This is a deeply personal account of teachers who have influenced the educational experience of Fergal Roche. Many of the wonderful characters we meet are those from Fergal's own experience of school and university. Others have taught his children, or are colleagues he has been privileged to work alongside throughout his career in education. As the book progresses we gain entertaining glimpses of Fergal's life, his foibles and talents, his wisdom about our profession. We even hear about his early celibacy and what he eats for breakfast...

Through Fergal's recollections of idiosyncratic teachers, lessons and the joy of sheer hard work through studying, we are taken on a journey that reflects his view of the key characteristics of successful teaching. His use of the art of story is powerful. Through Fergal's characterisation of teachers he reflects on why some of them helped him to learn and painfully relates his anger at those who unwittingly reversed his progress. He also reflects (sometimes critically) on his own experience as an English teacher and the ways he worked with his students to relentlessly demand from all of them more than they thought they could achieve.

Throughout the book we meet teachers who exhibit key skills of pedagogy that enable achievement of high academic standards. The majority of recollections relate to teachers during his secondary and university years. Interestingly, although these were teachers from Fergal's youth, many of the techniques described can now be related to pedagogical strategies endorsed by new research into cognitive science.

Almost all of the teachers are remembered for their subject knowledge, their intellectual academic engagement and their rigorous pursuit of excellence from their students. We meet inspirational colleagues such as Peter Hardwick, the English teacher who enthralled his pupils with his teaching of Evelyn Waugh. We hear about Geoff Hoare and his meticulous lesson preparation that enabled each lecture to be 'crafted to precision'. We hear stories of eccentricity, flashes of anger and unorthodox approaches that nevertheless proved to be effective in many cases.

Many of the teachers that Fergal introduces us to are almost fierce in their insistence that preparation for the lesson by the pupils must take place. There is no mention of 'flipped' or 'blended' learning but in essence setting homework that requires prior learning is exactly this. We read of the demanding study requirement demonstrated by teachers such as Jeremy Attlee who consequently 'let nothing fall between the cracks' and of others who tirelessly set homework that allowed students to prepare for the lesson ahead. Review of previous learning is described by Fergal as 'a bit like a snowball rolling down a hill: you went round and round covering the same things – and new things – again and again and steadily the snowball, or the learning, was enlarged'. This form of teaching incorporates modelling, deliberate and guided practice, memorisation and retrieval. He cites the effectiveness of this approach and has scant patience for those teachers who sought merely to entertain.

Modelling and scaffolding by the teacher is clearly illustrated in these classrooms. We meet teachers who insist on giving their pupils 'monstrous challenges' in the knowledge that through constant explanation, modelling and guided practice they will enable their pupils to achieve understanding. It is interesting to read of the tasks of eye-watering difficulty and insistence on high standards expected by teachers of their pupils. Affection and humour is also ever present. The anecdote about French teacher Brigid Hardwick and the invisible kitten is guaranteed to amuse.

Again and again we hear of teachers with extensive specialist knowledge who use skilful questioning and discussion to draw their students into compelling debate about literature. The importance of teacher expertise is clear, as is a methodology of teaching that refuses to accept that only the few will learn. This is teaching for all with the highest of expectations. Respect for these teachers is never in doubt. Even those who did little to engage their students, dedicated as they were to delivering their detailed notes while hardly looking up at the class, still hold a place in Fergal's appreciation of the deep insights they provided.

Organisation of knowledge, retrieval practice and memorisation through constant testing are all strategies deployed by many of the teachers. There is simply no room for failure. Often, the use of frequent testing as a means of ensuring that knowledge is embedded is a key strategy seen at work. Fergal reflects that in such classes the examination simply became an opportunity to demonstrate learning, as the teacher had established a knowledge framework that ensured every student knew what was expected of them. We hear much currently about the importance of high expectations for all pupils regardless of background or circumstance. The teachers introduced to us by Fergal all have the expectation that academic success is non-negotiable.

Importantly, the example of Colin Hall leading master-lessons for his colleagues at Holland Park comprehensive school provides recognition that teachers have a professional responsibility to mentor and learn from each other. My vision for the Chartered College of Teaching is that teachers will gain enhanced status and respect through seizing new opportunities to deepen their knowledge and expertise throughout their career.

This is a compelling book. As I read about these teachers I could not resist drawing parallels with my own experience as a pupil and student. I was caused to recall the teachers I had in school and at university and to recognise the skills and talents they demonstrated. I also thought of those who wasted my time or caused me to lose motivation or sense of purpose. Fergal is clear that the complexity of teaching is such that pursuit of perfection is fruitless. The teachers he recalls are often presented as eccentric and driven. However, it is the impact they have had on his learning that has qualified each of them to be included in this book. I hope you will enjoy these stories and that whilst reading, you aspire to be the kind of teacher that one day in the future might achieve the honour of being remembered with such reverence by one of your pupils.

Dame Alison Peacock
Chief Executive, Chartered College of Teaching

Introduction

I don't mean to be rude, but if you're an academic, you may now wish to pack up your things and leave. I'm afraid I'm not offering you any data analysis or survey findings or references to the theories of other academics.

If you work for the government, or are part of the government, then I'm not sure whether you should stay or not. I was going to write that, because I'm not about to unfold a series of evidence-based practices that I've seen working in classrooms around the land, you won't be interested. But then, looking at one or two policies that have crept back onto the government agenda recently, it seems that policy is no longer based on evidence in any case. See what you think. You know where the door is.

If you're a school leader, as I used to be, stay in the room. I hope you'll find this uncomfortable reading. The argument running through these short, anecdote-rich chapters, like a light current in a stream, is that our focus in schools over the last 20 years has been more about what goes on *outside* the classroom, than what goes on *inside*. The role of headteacher/principal has not been sufficiently focused on the art and skill of teaching, its subtleties, its huge challenges. The alchemy that takes place in schools happens in the interactions between teachers and pupils, and the learning experience teachers create. Rarely in the head's office, I'm afraid.

But if you're a teacher, were a teacher, or are thinking about becoming a teacher, I hope this book will be like coming to a party or, if you hate parties, doing something you really love. The message, in that light current, is that teaching is the most exciting and significant job in the world, hugely complex and exhausting, yes, but a role that needs to be mastered over decades of practice. *Mining for Gold* was the best metaphor I could come up with, but it's inadequate, really, because the potential that a teacher can unleash is actually far more valuable than gold. But anyway, I will give you stories of the many teachers I have come across who were really effective, despite their hugely different approaches. You will see that they are ordinary people who have produced an extraordinary impact.

Let me know what you think, via the email address quoted at the end of the book. Be encouraging.

I hope you'll find this an easy read. That's why I have kept each chapter short. Read one, think and muse. Enjoy.

Peter Hardwick – the inspirer

When I found out that I had been put in the A level English set taught principally by Mr Hardwick, I thought there must have been some mistake. I checked the list over and over. About 15 students, most of whom were people I regarded as geniuses (because they had all been in the top set in the run-up to O levels), were named. And me. Then I rationalised that my subject choices must have meant that the school had no option but to put me in this particular set. I certainly didn't *belong* with these others.

There wasn't any concept of 'student voice' in those days. You did as you were told. I had asked to do English, French and Spanish. But the list told me I was doing history instead of Spanish. Annoying, but I suppose they knew best. A friend of mine, who now runs a well-known school in Surrey, told me that he was told he was doing sciences for A level because the arts sets were getting too big. He had conceded without a murmur, as had I.

Peter Hardwick was venerated by his pupils and his reputation extended down through the school. He had an air of mystique about him. He was quietly spoken, extremely courteous, and other-worldly. He was a thinker: you'd pass him in the corridor and it was clear from the slightly eccentric smile on his face that to him, his delight was inside his head, and he was oblivious to the dull surroundings of the sixth form building, where his office was located.

He sat at his desk in front of the class. Took off his glasses. Shut his eyes and moved his hand over his face. 'Picture the scene. Remnants of a war-ravaged countryside over which a ray of light from the rising sun is casting its light…' We sit there in total silence, watching the epiphany happening in front of us. We are more like disciples than students as we are completely enthralled in the master's teaching. Evelyn Waugh's *Sword of Honour* trilogy comes alive. It was the moment when literature took on a three-dimensional existence for us. For a classroom of 16-year-old boys, most of whom found reading a torturous experience, a kind of transubstantiation was taking place as our minds were changed and our attitudes refashioned.

But Peter Hardwick wasn't your stereotypical dreamer, all starry-eyed vision and no substance. He was superbly well organised, worked incredibly hard and was the epitome of thoroughness. He took us through difficult passages in *Macbeth* and dictated (and obliged us to learn) a long-hand version of his own that explained every nuance in the speech, soliloquy or whatever. He must have spent hours preparing. He had endless bits of paper in front of him on which he had scrawled his notes about the literature we were studying. His filing system was, necessarily, highly effective, considering the number of different texts that we studied. He was intense, in a slightly intimidating way, and highly focused.

We were unclear for ages, when we began our A level studies, as to which books were on the curriculum and which were those that he simply insisted we were going to read. I seem to remember that much of the first half of term was taken up looking at Solzhenitsyn, each of us reading different novels and sharing our thinking. We wrote essays on different subjects. In fact, looking back, I think certain students were asked to read additional books and write up their thoughts. Anyone who showed a particular interest or ability was carefully nurtured and encouraged. I remember a friend, who like me had not been in the top sets for O level, enjoyed the Russian novel he had been given and volunteered to write a comparative study with one of the books on the syllabus. Mr Hardwick praised his efforts so much that my mate became a literature buff and ended up reading English at Oxford, largely because of the personalised tuition he had received, within the class, from his teacher. Looking back, it felt more as if we were at university than school. He'd throw out some thought or comment and wait for a response. He once read out some words in Italian and asked the class what the relevance was. I remember thinking how ridiculous it was that he could expect anyone to have a clue what he was talking about. Total silence. And then a muffled grunt of a response from the most dishevelled student in the class: 'They are the opening words from Dante's *Inferno*.' The whole class turned in awe. More and more students (sadly, not me, at the time) were clearly beginning to read extensively in their free time. Peter Hardwick had ignited a spark that was already turning into a flame for several of my classmates.

He'd spend half a lesson, when he handed back our books, pointing out what he had liked in our work and reading out examples of particularly incisive comment from one student or another. I remember how much I wanted to please him and would take any nugget of praise and cherish it dearly. Once we were studying some kind of satirical poetry and for homework had to write a poem of our own. I poked fun at one of the Jesuit priests who taught us history. I can't remember what mark I got, but it was encouraging. What I do remember is the comment alongside it. The handwriting was obscure. It could either have read: 'You have the trick' or 'you have the truth'. I analysed it over and over but couldn't figure out which was the more accurate reading. Only later did I realise that my teacher was deliberately putting to use the ambiguity that handwriting affords, in a context where hidden meaning was exactly what we were studying. I have thought about the cleverness and humour of that comment for years. It shows something of the hidden depths of a man who was so greatly respected, despite his unassuming demeanour.

I ended up studying English at university. When I eventually became an English teacher, I spent hours preparing what I wanted to teach. I marked books thoroughly and created something of a ritual in the way I handed back the books and encouraged my pupils. I tried to pass on the love for literature I had gained over the years since my interest had been sparked by Peter Hardwick.

But I never really gained the same passion as he had. As a student, you wanted what he had. He saw depths in what he read that we too wanted to reach. He encountered ideas and nuances that mesmerised him, and he made us jealous of the journeys that he was travelling in front of us.

He died in 2013. He had spent 40 years in the classroom and, although he had a very significant role in overseeing university applications, he had carried on with a significant teaching responsibility. His work had a lasting impact. Mark Thompson, the chief executive of the *New York Times* and former director general of the BBC, wrote an obituary in the *Guardian* (28th February 2013) in which he described Peter as an English teacher of exceptional brilliance and inspiration.

Peter Hardwick had a profound impact on my development as a teacher. If I had realised then how significant my time with him was to be, I would have applied myself with more diligence. Never mind. It happened, and I was lucky to be there.

The teaching itch

My parents told me that when I was very young I used to line up my two younger siblings, along with a couple of friends, and hand out work for them to do. I would then give them feedback, which might include detention. What they didn't tell me was what my classroom management was like or whether I had optimised behaviour for learning.

At school I did a lot of organising. I ran 'Mastermind' competitions (mainly so I could be the quizmaster) and put together indoor football leagues that proved popular. Before university I had worked as a teaching assistant in three different schools. And I loved it. In my last year at school, though, I applied to study law and was offered a place at Birmingham (grades of BBC required) and Southampton (BB or BCC). In the end I turned both down and instead began training to become a Jesuit priest, entering the 'novitiate' on 8th September. I'll tell you about this episode later in the book. But just to whet your appetite, it includes working in a hostel for the homeless where I became infected with lice (I never told my mother this), and walking across the neck of Spain on pilgrimage, surviving on £1 per day.

When I eventually got to university, I directed lots of plays, including the big annual Gilbert and Sullivan musical in the professional theatre on the Exeter University campus. I loved bringing people together in a common enterprise and I particularly enjoyed getting individuals to perform better than they thought they could. Even then I think I saw people's potential in ways that excited me, something that came to be a central feature of my teaching career.

But with my last year at university approaching, I couldn't make up my mind whether I wanted to go into business or into teaching. I was offered a place by PWC to take up an accountancy training position, one of the generic routes into business. However, in the autumn term I saw an advert for a job in a prep school which offered the chance to teach English to five classes in years 7 and 8, run the library, coach rugby and cricket, direct the school play, sing in the school choir and edit the school magazine. It looked like heaven and I spent a few hours putting together an application that I knew would be speculative, because the job title was 'head of English' and they were unlikely to give it to someone straight from university, even though I was 25 by then. I couldn't hide my enthusiasm when I was shown round the school by the deputy. It took weeks before I found out whether or not I had got the job. I rang the school and the secretary hauled the head out of lunch to tell me that I had been successful. I whooped with delight. I subsequently found out that the school offered tied accommodation in a block of flats next door. By then I was engaged to a fellow student and could see how we might actually afford to get married soon after we graduated, even though my salary, in 1986, was only to be £8,000.

I loved teaching English. I could choose whatever books and poems I wanted to teach and could be as ambitious as I wanted. Even though the school was very posh, I took pupils to see plays by David Hare, the left-leaning playwright, to broaden their minds. We studied literature from the developing world and attempted to copy the way Shakespeare wrote. I insisted that each class 'jabbered' for two minutes at the start of each class. They had extra exercise books for this, and *jabbering* meant writing non-stop, with no pausing, putting down on the page whatever was in your head. The whole point was to develop confidence in getting words onto a page, something that many 12- and 13-year-olds do not have. Good behaviour won points for the class. Sloppy behaviour gave points to me. Each half-term we would work out who had won. If it was the class, they were given a lesson to do what they liked (and I think I might have thrown in some Mars bars). Losing meant a lesson of detention, when I took away the free time that the rest of the school was enjoying at the time. I wanted the library to be treated as an oasis of silence and was ruthless in punishing pupils who didn't adhere to this. They soon got the point. I would read my own book during the weekly library lesson and would talk to them about it at other points during the week. They needed to see adults reading and I tried to be a worthy role model in this regard.

A teacher could make a lot of progress with children of that age, when they were so impressionable and open to new ideas. It was such a joy to see a number of pupils come to feel confident in writing meaningful sentences and understanding complex writing. I remember how hard I worked with a couple of them in particular and, at times, felt like tearing my hair out because the progress seemed so slow. Perhaps my most difficult pupil surprised me more than any other. He seemed slow and pedantic in the way he approached the subject, but he was always cheerful and willing to put up with the hassle I gave him on a daily basis. One of the great things about teaching English, by the way, is that you tend to teach the same class a good number of times each week so that you get to know your pupils really well. I certainly got to know this particular character well. I still remember his handwriting at the time, which meandered very roughly along the line of the exercise book, getting smaller and smaller as it made its way. And it took forever to emerge from the pen, like squeezing honey out of a surgical needle. In the end, he managed to pass really tough exams into his next school. Years later he rowed alongside Steve Redgrave in an Olympic boat, winning a number of gold medals and is now a partner in a law company. I am proud that I had some small part in his development, helping him through a time in his life when he struggled. That is, of course, when teachers have their maximum impact, as they coach and cajole their charges when they are doubtful of their own capability.

After a year or so of teaching, I started a master's degree with the Open University. I remember it being very demanding, with loads of reading of academically dense texts, a sizeable assignment every few weeks, a week of lectures every summer at a university campus, and exams in October. It deepened my understanding and interest in language and literacy, which I translated back into the classroom.

At least ten years after I had been teaching, I was standing outside a country church on Christmas Day after the service when I received a tap on the shoulder. I turned to face a guy in his early twenties who was about six foot three and a good 15 stone. He said, 'Hello, Sir. I bet you don't remember me.' I scrutinised him for a few seconds and hazarded a guess. Correct. He told me that when he was about 12 I was furious with him for a piece of work he had done. I made him stand up in front of the class and told him that he was one of the cleverest pupils I had taught but was completely wasting his talent. I had made him redo the piece of work and I threatened him that if he didn't eventually get top A level results and get to a leading university, I would find out where he lived and come and taunt him. I realise now that what I had said, and the way had I said it, was probably not the epitome of professionalism, but I was young and inexperienced at the time and, come on, I meant well. Anyway, he said that he had got three As at A level and gone to Imperial College, got a first-class honours degree and was about to start a master's. He didn't actually thank me for my historic outburst. In fact, I think he just wanted to make sure that I scratched him off the naughty list that so many children think teachers keep tucked away for later use. I congratulated him, and he looked relieved.

Talking of naughty lists, a famous England cricketer by the name of Ashley Giles visited the secondary school where he had studied and where I have been a governor for years. The head told me that Ashley didn't seem that relaxed, considering that he must have been one of the more famous alumni of the school. After a while, the head asked him if he was alright, as he clearly seemed agitated. He admitted that he couldn't shake off the anxiety he felt, as he knew that the deputy head he owed a punishment essay to was still at the school. The head went and got the deputy to assure Ashley that he was now off the hook.

Experiences like that are not common for teachers, but they remind them of the extraordinary influence they can have on the lives of their students for many years. One of my son's friends at university had been taught at school by a close friend of mine. She had loads of stories about him, admired him hugely and was delighted that my son knew him. It is amazing how closely children observe their teachers, clearly noting their idiosyncrasies, their habits, their drive. And they recognise teachers who have helped them.

Jeremy Attlee –
the completer-finisher

Mr Attlee was one of the most organised teachers I have come across in my education to date. Just to look at him, you could guess this: smart jacket and tie, neatly pressed trousers, shined shoes. I remember his handwriting. He was left-handed and used Pentels – green plastic with a healthy flow of ink. He formed his letters in that round cursive style so popular with teachers even today.

I admired him. He wasn't your typical confident, outgoing character we so often expect teachers to be. Instead, he was especially shy, had a bit of a nervous twitch and a problem with eczema. Of course, with his name, he inevitably became known as Clem, after the post-war prime minister who affronted Churchill by stealing the country from him with a 12% swing from Conservative to Labour (the largest ever achieved in a general election), giving Labour the first majority government it had ever had. He was in fact related to him: his grandfather, Tom, was Clem's brother and one of the 16,000 men who had registered as conscientious objectors during World War I. It was a bold move on Tom's part, which had a significant impact on his whole life. His professional life as an architect never recovered and he moved to Cornwall to escape the continuing slating he received in London. He was determined to hold fast to his stance as a Christian socialist. And I was taught by his grandson!

So, Jeremy came from an impressive line of strong-willed individuals. Not that he came across as someone who might ever venture into public life or make some bold gesture of defiance himself. He worked in a school in the middle of nowhere, had a tiny room with shoddy amenities, and was assistant year head of what would now be called year 7, meaning he had loads of administrative tasks to complete on top of his teaching.

He taught French, Spanish and (I think) Latin. He had an encyclopaedic knowledge of his subject, was fascinated by the etymology of words and the culture they sprang from. He was very much a textbook-led teacher, but as I recall, they were well-put-together textbooks, and pushed you through the grammar of the language at a considerable speed. I had opted to take Spanish as an extra subject for the two years leading to O levels. I think it meant missing a bit of free time. I can't remember why I opted to do so, but I was pretty good at French and Latin and enjoyed figuring out how to put a language together. Jeremy's lessons weren't exciting affairs, but you had a strong sense of progress. He gave us homework exercises and vocabulary learning to do each week. There was always a test, which I enjoyed for its competitive value. But learning a language from scratch and being expected to get a good grade at O level in two years was a tall order.

I distinctly remember getting to the point early in my second year of studying Spanish where I had little confidence that I would ever get to the stage of competently handling an oral exam or of being able to write free prose in the language. I waited behind to speak to Mr Attlee after the lesson. I was a boy of 15 who was enormously lacking in confidence. Others in the class I rated highly and compared myself unfavourably. Several had won top scholarships to the school. One boy, John Armour (now Professor of Genetics at Nottingham University, with degrees from both Oxford *and* Cambridge), seemed to have a photographic memory. I could never understand how his concentration could be so intense after we had all been out on a rugby pitch in a Lancastrian winter for an hour, less than 30 minutes before the lesson. He seemed to look at a list of vocabulary and learn the words instantly. I was thick by comparison and would never be able to achieve like that. I might as well give up there and then. I spoke to Mr Attlee and asked him if it would be better to stop wasting his time and give up now. I was never going to get grades anything like those of the others. He told me that I was doing fine, that all I needed to do was to carry on with how I was working and I would gradually feel more confident. I shouldn't worry. He would help me.

The fact that I still remember his words emphasises their significance. I must have trusted him, because I put my head down and got on with it. I ended up with a B, which in those days meant that I had come in something like the top 20-30% of candidates across the board; no mean feat. I remember my Spanish oral, being asked what my pastimes were. I got half-way through a sentence where I was trying to explain where I played cricket and realising that I had no idea what the Spanish for 'cricket pitch' was. I came out with *'hay cesped y aqui jugamos cricket'* – literally, 'there is some grass and here we play cricket'. The examiner burst out laughing and I didn't know whether to join him or cry. Anyway, it shows that I had become quite ballsy by the time it came to the exam.

Lessons with Mr Attlee were spent checking through all the basics: going through the tense covered in that chapter, testing our learning of the vocabulary, trying some of the exercises to see how much we understood. I never asked a question in class as it would show up my ineptitude in front of all the bright kids, but questions would be asked about some aspect of the text we were looking at, all of which revolved around living in Spain. Mr Attlee loved thinking about the differences in behaviour, for example, between young people in Madrid and young people in the UK and the discussions were engaging.

His approach to teaching was not glamorous, but it was extremely thorough. He let nothing fall between the cracks. He explained the grammar. You learned it. He tested you. You learned the vocab. He tested you. You moved on to the next chapter. He kept testing you on previous chapters, so you couldn't forget what you had learned. It was a bit like a snowball rolling down a hill: you went round and round, covering the same things – and new things – again and again, and steadily the snowball, or the learning, was enlarged. He always marked our books thoroughly, pointing out every mistake and writing out a phrase to copy, if we had misunderstood. I used to be annoyed by teachers who spent weeks before they handed back work. You always knew that Mr

Attlee would have done the work, however busy he might have been, and we respected him for that. In fact, considering how shy he was, he was amazingly well respected by the pupils. I think there was a sort of contract between us: 'I'll do my bit as the teacher; you do the work I set, thoroughly. Result: you will succeed.' Not a bad formula.

Missionary zeal

Much to the shock of my friends and family, for several days during the Easter holidays before my A levels I attended an assessment to be accepted for training to become a Jesuit priest. A couple of weeks later I received a letter to say I had been accepted and should show up at the training house in Birmingham on 8th September. I sent off my cancellation vouchers to UCCA, the University Central Council for Admissions, as it was in those days. I remember that the vouchers saying you were turning down the places you had been offered had black diagonal lines across them, as if they were wearing black armbands and you should be in mourning. So, I had given up my places to study law at leading universities and instead was going to embrace a life of service and sacrifice. Was I totally off my rocker?

Jesuits embrace a life where you try to follow the example set by Jesus as closely as possible. For starters, you commit yourself to a life of poverty (you don't own anything of your own), chastity (no sex, no exclusive relationships) and obedience (you'll do what you're told and go where you're told to go). Jesuits commit to not accepting 'preferment' (promotion, in effect) within the church unless the pope specifically commands it. Pope Francis, ironically, was a Jesuit. I say 'was', because when you are ordered to become a bishop, you effectively leave the organisation. As a way of life, it's pretty total.

The first two-year period is called 'novitiate', when you are a novice and go through the early part of training, which the Jesuits called 'formation', to indicate that it goes much deeper than simply giving you skills: it is forming your mindset and your attitude. I still remember the regime I underwent when in Birmingham. Up at 6, an hour's meditation between 6.30 and 7.30, Mass until about 8.05. Breakfast in silence. 'Indoor works', which meant doing the cleaning you were responsible for. Any time you had spare was supposed to go into studying, which involved the Jesuit constitution, New Testament Greek, the gospels, a bit of basic theology. At about 11.45 you had a session lasting about 50 minutes, when one of the priests lectured you. At 12.45 you made your 'examen', which you did twice a day and involved going over the past half-day to consider how you had lived up to your calling as a disciple of Christ.

Lunch will amuse you. You wore your gown, a black, cassock-like affair with extra pieces of material that were called 'wings'. Two novices were on duty each week for preparing the dining room and washing up. They acted as waiters during lunch. Another's role was to read. While everyone stood up in front of their place, the novice master (the guy in charge) said grace and blessed the food. We sat down and a short reading from one of the gospels was given. When that finished, the serving could begin. Then the lector would continue reading from a book designed to edify us. While I was there, for example, we had *Mere Christianity* by C S Lewis, amongst a number of others. That would carry on until we got to the end of the second course (yes, I put on weight). The 'socius' (don't you just love these words), who was a priest whose role was to assist the novice master, would thank the reader, who would then say, 'It follows in the same chapter', and the novice master would say something like '*Deo gratias*', meaning 'thanks be to God'. We were then allowed to speak.

There was no dishwasher, so 30 people's plates, glasses, cutlery had to be washed up by hand in an enormous sink. If you were the cook's assistant, as I was for four or five months at one stage, you did all the kitchen washing up for all three meals each day.

After lunch we went to the chapel for five minutes to pray for our benefactors, the people whose charitable contributions to the Society ('the Jesuits' is the nickname for the Society of Jesus) were paying for us to live. Then we had a break for about half an hour before turning up for 'outdoor works', which essentially meant gardening for an hour and a half. Not something I particularly enjoyed. Then a shower, tea and a bit of cake before rushing to afternoon studies, which might be the Greek lesson (which I actually liked: in year one, we were taught by an impassioned American lady who loved the subject; and in year two, by a retired Jesuit priest who had been a leading scholar in Rome and who had loads of stories to tell) or occasionally we would have a series of lectures given by a visitor. For one week, I remember we learned to type for three hours each day and by the time we finished I could do about 50 words a minute, which has stood me in good stead ever since (like right now, as I am writing this, for instance). After that, we had to fit in half an hour's spiritual reading and half an hour's meditation before supper at 7.30, consisting of a cooked meal plus bread and jam. Then you could watch telly, chat or relax. At some stage you needed to prepare your meditation for the following morning and maybe do a bit more studying. At 10 there would be Compline, a service in the chapel lasting about 15 minutes. Finally we entered the *magnum silencium* during which we were expected to be quiet, until after breakfast the following day. On Thursday afternoons we played football rather than do outdoor works and on Saturday we went out on a day trip and took sandwiches with us. Sundays were pretty dull, with little formal structure to them. We were expected to attend Mass at one of the many churches in Birmingham, to be with 'the people of God'.

This regime would last for two or three months, and a few days before we left, a notice would be pinned up on the board telling us where we would be going for our next 'experiment'. This was a six-week test (based on the Latin word, *experimentum* meaning 'test') where we put our learning to the test in practical settings. While I was there, people worked in prisons, hostels for the homeless, parishes in deprived neighbourhoods, and all of us made a pilgrimage across the top of Spain subsisting on £1 a day. I spent one of my experiments working as a nursing auxiliary in a hospice for the terminally ill and watched three people die during the six weeks I was there. That was quite something for an 18-year-old to cope with, and I found myself growing up quickly and stepping out of the privileged cocoon in which I had grown up. I remember the pilgrimage well. I was put with a laid-back friendly guy by the name of Michael Kirwan, who is now a theology professor. At some time in April we were dropped by the side of an A road in Birmingham and wished well. We hitch-hiked down to Exeter on the first day and pitched our tent in a field somewhere near the motorway. It was a freezing night and I hardly slept a wink. When we emerged from our sleeping bags the next day we found a two-foot snow drift on one side and the landscape outside entirely white. We eventually got a lift to Plymouth, from where we were going to catch our ferry, from a very well-spoken individual who owned an estate and had been travelling to pick up new peacocks… as you do. We discovered afterwards, through a process of deduction, that our cheerful driver had been the Earl of Iddesleigh. Six weeks later we got back to Birmingham, having walked about 150 miles, with some very colourful and amusing stories that still keep me going, even today.

Going through tough experiences and reflecting on them (the Jesuits made an art form of the business of reflecting on experience) helped me grow up. I learned a lot about myself, what I was good at and what I shied away from. At the end of the two years the three of us who remained, out of the ten who had started, made our vows (poverty, chastity, obedience) and travelled to Dublin where we all began our studies in philosophy, the next step on the journey towards ordination as a priest in the Society of Jesus. After a few months I had a nasty football injury which required an operation and several weeks' convalescence. During this time I came to the realisation that at some stage in the future I would want to get married and have a family. I arranged to leave the Jesuits and made my way back to my family home in Bristol. I applied for a university place at Exeter and was accepted to study English and Education, a four-year course.

I had wanted to give my whole life to something that would be significant and lasting, not ephemeral and transient. Life has meaning and I wanted to discover what that was about so that I could pass it on to others. Although I ended up leaving the Jesuits, I don't think that fundamental desire ever changed for me.

Geoff Hoare – the enthusiast

By the time I got to university, I'd had enough of Chaucer: stories of friars and nun's priests and endless chatter about a confined world written in a language difficult to understand. So when it came to deciding on second-year options in my English course, I ticked the 'anything but Chaucer' box. And somehow that meant I was put down for 18th century literature, something I had never looked at before. When I stared at the letter from the university (this was pre-email) confirming my options, I wondered what the course would entail. All I could think of was the Scarlet Pimpernel, men in white wigs, large ladies in long dresses with thrusting décolletage getting drunk. I'm not sure where all these images came from, and whether they held any validity whatsoever, but they didn't get me overly excited. I can't remember if we were given any pre-reading. In fact, when you read what I'm about to tell you, I think we can conclude that nothing was handed out beforehand.

So: day one of the course. The lecture is in a part of the university I haven't been to before. I have always wondered what was in this particular building. I don't even know which of my friends *have* opted for this course. I mosey down the corridor looking for E186. The door is open and there is music playing. It is like going into an art studio or a converted warehouse, with lots of bare stone and wooden beams. The ceilings are really high. The windowsills are wide and there is a counter running around the walls, as in an old-fashioned science lab. Fabric is stretched over parts of the room and various artefacts are displayed. The music is chamber, very precise, highly structured with repetitive themes. Coffee and cake are being handed out as we come through the door. The lecturer, whom I have never met before, is at the front welcoming people and introducing himself as if we are coming to some kind of sophisticated soirée or something. One or two people are staring around the room and he tells them where the various bits and pieces have come from. He mentions the music, when and by whom it was written, and the circumstances they were in at the time.

After ten minutes or so, 'Call me' Geoff wonders whether we would like to take a seat. We do so. He tells us how delighted he is that we have chosen this particular course. He talks about his fascination with the period we are studying and how its literature tells us so much about the major ideas running through society at the time. He tells a story about a couple of the pieces of art he has brought in, where they come from and why they are significant. He talks about the music and the situation the composer was in when he wrote it. Then he puts a few slides up on the screen. They are of gardens. They are highly organised, full of symmetry, circular ponds with tall fountains, paths creating a matrix of converging lines, on a huge scale, immaculate in their precise structure. Question: where are these gardens? A couple of us hazard a guess at Versailles. Correct. Another picture comes up of another garden. Where? No one guesses correctly. Answer: they are only a couple of hours away from where we are now sitting. Designed at the same time as Versailles. He points out that the physical landscape of the country we are now living in would be significantly different if it weren't for the work of talented individuals and their patrons from the period we are considering.

Why were 18th century gardens in France and gardens in the South-West of England so similar? Why so highly structured? What similarities do the gardens and the music that has been playing have?

The questions are left hanging. We are asked if we know anything about the major dramas in England at the time. We suggest: fear about revolution spreading from France; fear about Catholics trying to take the country back to a time when the Pope was considered more important than the sovereign. What else? What did people do for entertainment? How could they express their opinions? How did they flirt and show off their wares to each other? How did they establish their status?

We look at language and the way prose and poetry was constructed at the time. What had come in the previous century? How was that time different from the period we are studying? So what did the iambic pentameter mean? Who used it? Ah, Shakespeare, yes. And how might he have been considered by his successors a hundred years later?

So, through a series of questions, we are led into the life of Alexander Pope and the world he inhabited. We are told about his situation, a Catholic nobleman barred from voting or holding any kind of political or public office, whose offspring are ineligible from attending the great universities, who is taxed extra for not attending Church of England services on Sundays. Who is he in society? Does he have any status and, if so, how does he establish and assert his identity?

The session is two hours long and it flashes by. Half-way through, we stop, listen to some more music and have some more coffee. We return to our seats and are told about *The Rape of the Lock* and how and why it was one of the subtlest forms of sedition ever produced in English literature. We are told of its genius, of how it followed all the form and structure that was expected at the time on the surface but contained revolution underneath, if you knew where to look. It spoke one thing to the establishment, another to the constrained Catholic landowning class.

We are handed sheets with a poem written at the same time as Pope's epic. We are asked to read it, digest it, hear it inside our heads. Geoff tells us that it is like limbering up for a run or a game of football. We need to get our minds ready for what is to come. We are told that we need to analyse the poem and write about what we see and understand and feel. If we do a good job, then next week he will give us the books containing the verse we are going to study, but only when we are prepared for it.

We are challenged, focused, geed up.

Geoff's session was masterfully planned. His room was designed like the set of a play. He had the audio-visual input carefully thought through. Our two hours were crafted to precision, even though they appeared so laid back. He teased us with the literature and wouldn't let us have it 'til we'd proved ourselves. He mixed questioning, informing, listening. He made us work hard, although we enjoyed it so we didn't notice the effort required. But, I hear you say, learners can't enjoy everything they study, for goodness' sake. But our subject matter was, on the face of it, hundreds of lines of dry dusty poetry. How can you enjoy it? But we did. It was presented to us as an unfolding drama and we couldn't get enough of it.

Interestingly, he worked part-time. It must have taken him hours to prepare.

That course was the first *first* I achieved at university. I got so excited by the subject matter (pages and pages of iambic pentameter – not at all sexy to look at) that I worked my butt off and achieved an A for every essay.

I leave the room smiling, leave the building, enter the quad and bump into a friend who has just come from the Chaucer session. 'How did it go?' I ask. 'Hmm,' she replies.

Learning from others

I wanted to copy everything I loved about the teachers who had made a difference to me. By the time I started in the classroom I was very much in favour of being tough on kids and demanding superb output from them. I was definitely anti-liberal and, looking back, too much so. I had found some of the lecturers on my teacher-training course to be so keen on empathising with children's difficulties that being rigorous or demanding was clearly not the default position they envisaged for us. Everything seemed to be about understanding the child, starting by assuming every child wants to learn. They don't. They want an easy life. Well, at least that's what I thought at the time. The truth, of course, is greatly more nuanced than that.

I loved books, poems, writing, speaking, acting, directing plays. Teaching English was a huge amount of fun. My early years of teaching relied much more on copying some of my best teachers than it ever did on putting into practice what I had learned from teacher trainers. I had done part of my teacher training in the US, where I'd had a 'master teacher', a woman in her early thirties who had been a lawyer for a few years before retraining. She was highly organised, knew exactly what concepts and skills she wanted to teach, and refused to let the kids get away with anything. The main employer for the families we served was one of the largest penitentiaries in the US, and the children's parents mostly had something to do with it, reluctantly or otherwise. They were mostly white working-class country kids. My teacher believed they could achieve as much as any other children and she drummed that belief into me, too.

I liked the whole notion of teacher as apprentice. My master teacher would teach a lesson. We would discuss what she was trying to get the students to learn and how effective we thought the actual lesson had been. Then I would teach the same lesson with a different class in the same year group. Sometimes I would teach a lesson that she had prepared and sometimes she would teach from what I had prepared. We would compare notes as to what had been more effective. It meant I learnt quickly because I was constantly getting feedback. She was in the room most of the time, watching, taking notes. She made sure I got to know the other teachers in the English department, that I watched them teach, that I found out what kind of lives they lived. She wanted me to get a good feel for what living and breathing as a teacher felt like.

But I was full of zeal rather than subtlety in my early years of teaching and I wish I had spent more time watching older, more experienced teachers who used a greater variety of approaches. Several times during my US teaching practice, we went to watch teachers in other schools. I still remember one who taught English to the *senior* year (high schools and universities in the US follow four-year courses and divide into freshman, sophomore, junior, senior years). She wandered into the room with a cup of coffee in her hand and yelled at the 30-or-so students milling around the room: 'Ok, bears, to your places.' She proceeded to summarise, via a Q&A session, what they had been learning in the previous few lessons. Then she picked out a few highlights in the 'papers' that she had marked and got really excited by the insights that students had developed about the text being studied. They were going very deep into the literature. She was ambitious, and she took the best analysis from the students and led them deeper. It was fascinating to watch, and a bit like observing a talented artist putting together a picture, beginning with rudimentary lines and ending with depth and colour. She allowed a lot of looseness in the discussion, but somehow got the students to realise that, collectively, they were reaching a level of intricacy in their understanding that they didn't consider possible. I don't think I ever managed that in my own teaching, possibly because I only taught for little more than a decade.

When I became a governor of a large secondary school a few years ago, I asked if, rather than be given the 'show' tour around the school by the head, I could watch a few lessons taken by those teachers who they considered to be most consistently outstanding. I visited five or six lessons. By far the most impressive individual was a music teacher in her late fifties, teaching year 9s (14-year-olds) about jazz: its origins, form, relationship with classical music and leading exponents. Every student seemed to be concentrating intensely. Chris, the teacher, had one part of the class working with A level students on a talk they were going to present, another was analysing a short piece of music and another was trying to compose a short song. I was struck by how engaged they were in a subject that many young people would consider enigmatic these days. Throughout the lesson, Chris was telling me how well each group was doing in terms of their understanding. She was very clear as to where they needed to get to by the end of the lesson and kept checking to ensure they were going to arrive. Leaving one group to sixth-formers was a risk. Would they be effective or would they wander off task? She was making sure that they too were teaching effectively. It would be interesting to see if any of them end up going into the profession themselves, as their lesson was impressive.

When I became a head in the school where I had already been a teacher, the first thing I did, to try and encourage a lot of staff who had been there for decades, was to ask them to go and watch each other teach. I myself was amazed that in a school where there were only about 25 teachers, there could be such a variety of practice. Some were highly structured in their approach, with every part of the lesson having its own purpose and loads of pupil activity; others were inspirational and fascinating as they explained an area of their subject; others got pupils to copy what they themselves were doing before branching out on their own; others explained the concept to be covered and immediately tested the children's understanding of it. In amongst all of that was lots of highly effective teaching which, when distilled, could act as a core for improving the school as a whole.

But some thought this approach rather insulting. One told me that he had been to teacher training college and had been an effective teacher for nearly 20 years. Why did he need to watch others? I realised that what seemed so obviously beneficial from my perspective could be seen to be undermining from that of others. It took a considerable amount of time before it became anything like normal practice for teachers to work together. I made the fundamental mistake of insisting that teachers observed each other and wrote reports on their observations, to prove to me that they had done it. Thus it became yet another chore and made the job less enjoyable: the exact opposite of what I wanted. I could have won hearts and minds by starting with just a few teachers who were keen to get involved and to have them share what they had seen and learned. That way, it wouldn't have come across as a management demand, but as something which could have significant benefits to the individual teachers. I excuse myself now by remembering that I was only in my early thirties at the time and thought that logic prevailed over all else when it came to managing and leading. As someone told me in an interview for the Director of Education role in a multi-academy trust recently, it is pointless to try and achieve real change until you have won the hearts and minds of those you want to change. That usually entails a longer and much more sophisticated approach. I think I'm better at it these days, although I still want everything to be done in a hurry, which annoys my colleagues.

One of the reasons that teaching was so diverse in the school where I got my first headship was that we had two French-curriculum classes, taught by native French teachers. Even though France is only 30 miles across the Channel, its education culture is completely different. It is more akin to China than it is to England. The emphasis is on the teacher's ability to explain the subject matter set out in the textbook, which is approved by the ministry. Teachers are instructors first and foremost. They are the big brains at the front of the class: the greater their knowledge of their subject, the more they are paid. This is so different from the UK, where the teacher's role is to ensure learning is taking place in the most effective and efficient way possible. How that happens is down to the teacher. The French approach is much more homogeneous, in that their teachers will be much more similar in their practice than English teachers are in theirs. Having the chance to look closely at the two approaches was fascinating for me. The French children worked harder than the English, but were less enamoured of their time in the classroom, I would say. I don't think there were huge differences in the learning outcomes when we did the occasional comparative study.

Culture in UK teaching has changed a lot in the last decade or so and teachers are used to people coming in and out of their classroom in a way that they certainly weren't in the '90s. Now we have trios of teachers who work together, and 'lesson study', where teachers are involved in collaboratively planning, teaching, observing and analysing learning and teaching in 'research lessons'. In an age where we have to be more and more efficient in getting children to master their learning in the shortest possible time, we need to learn from each other and not remain isolated in the way that kept teachers happy in times past. No longer do the most effective teachers place such a high premium on independence and autonomy. They realise that others can plan better than they can, some are better at explaining particular concepts, others are experts at assessment. By sharing in this way, perhaps teaching can become a manageable profession, where people are quite happy to stay for their entire working lives and not leave when they have made their four-year 'sacrifice' on behalf of the nation.

Terry Brooks – the enforcer

My younger brother got a top scholarship to Oxford to study classics at a very prestigious college. He says that he learnt more Latin and Greek in the three years when he was taught by Terry Brooks – between the ages of about 9 and 12 – than in any of the subsequent five or so years before he went to university.

If a teacher's walk, dress, body language, teaching style and voice were all seen to be strong indicators of teacher effectiveness, Terry would have had a big red cross next to his name in the inspector's mark book. He typically arrived several minutes late for lessons, often with his shirt out. We were scared stiff of him. Although he was only average height, he had a booming, deep bass Welsh voice and he could make the room shake with a sudden vocal explosion. He had eyes everywhere and could spot in seconds if he didn't have your full attention. I should also say, though, that lots of things amused him and occasionally he couldn't hide a smile because he found what one of us had said or done to be so bizarre. We realised, even then, that he was a real human and not some kind of scary machine. In terms of lesson planning, there didn't seem to be any. He carried a copy of L A Wilding's *Latin Course for Schools,* the textbook widely used at the time, and he would often ask us at the start of the lesson which chapter we were on. For ages, I have tried to figure out how he could have been so effective with so many pupils over so many years and how the head who appointed him could have recognised his talent when he appointed him. In fact, I think Terry might have been appointed solely on the basis that he had played rugby in the (I think) Swansea University first team and therefore, of course, he could coach the game. Obvious.

We moved at pace through the lessons. He would explain how a bit of grammar worked and immediately give us a sentence to translate (often from English into Latin, which we didn't realise is considered to be a lot harder than the other way around). As soon as we had done it, we queued up in front of his desk to find out whether we had got it right. If we had, he immediately gave us something a bit harder to do. Once we had all been up and got it right, he explained on the board what we had been struggling with. He would then take a set of exercises and go around the room getting us to answer them. It was hard work and probably the most tiring lesson of the day.

He also taught us Roman history as part of the Latin syllabus, but most of our learning in this regard was based on the stories read to us by a teacher two years previously. Terry took us through exam questions from years and years of past papers and we discussed as a class what the right or best answers were. We were all pretty competitive and enjoyed nailing the answers quickly and earning some tiny snippet of praise, which was not in plentiful supply.

There were endless tests, either just orally around the room or on paper. You were expected to know and remember everything. He was constantly going over previous ground. He loved picking up a completely different book, Kennedy's *Latin Primer,* and seeing if he could catch us out on anything. I realise now that we were a bit like snowballs rolling down the hill. We were making progress, but constantly going round again to cover ground. Looking back, it was rigorous and effective.

Exercise books were used as work books to test our understanding of whatever element of the language we were studying. We didn't slave through reams and reams of exercises and Terry didn't, as far as I remember, do much marking. I recall that we would compare where we were up to as a class, in the textbook, compared with the other class in our year. When we moved onto Book Two, we felt a great sense of achievement.

All feels a bit humdrum? Well, the outcomes weren't. Students from his classes won numerous prizes and scholarships and exhibitions, or whatever they were called, from the senior schools eager to attract sparky individuals into the mix of their intakes. We developed a thorough grounding in the subject. Today, the trendy term might be *mastery*.

He constantly put you under pressure as a pupil. You were taught something, then you had to use it. Your brain hurt. He taught you some more. You used it. You'd go round the class attempting the next challenging sentence in a translation. 'Where's the verb?' he would bark, '... and what's the subject? What declension is that? Correct. And if it's the subject, what case is it? If it happened to be the object, what would it be?' His questioning joined together acres of learning that we had done over the previous weeks. In cognitive development terms, it must have opened up more neural pathways than any other subject we were studying at the time.

So, something highly effective was going on, but it was well masked. To the outsider looking for *correctness*, this was a teacher who shouted at his pupils, who pushed them almost to the point of aggression, who insisted that every person in the room understood the subject matter and could prove their understanding.

A friend of mine runs a leading independent grammar school within the famous Edward VI foundation set up in the 16th century. We have had many conversations as to how much freedom to allow teachers. He argues that you should deliberately afford them a great deal of scope. Often these teachers are the ones with the loudest and most critical voices in the staffroom, the ones who often can make life difficult for the senior leadership. I don't know exactly what happened with Terry, but he ended up leaving after a big falling-out with the deputy head, an erstwhile friend. Things at the school calmed down after a period of tension, but I can't help thinking that the students missed out. There was something of the genius about him and he refused to contemplate that any student could in any way fail to understand what many thought was a fiendishly difficult subject. He had a huge effect on my own teaching in subsequent years, as I pushed my students hard (sometimes, I now admit, a bit too hard perhaps) and refused to allow any to slip through the net. At the time, I drew quite a bit of criticism from a few other colleagues (particularly the Latin teacher, as I recall) that I was unreasonable. But I think I'd fit in well with today's no-excuses approach, which insists that teachers never limit the expectations they make of their charges.

Once, when Terry was late for a lesson, we (very dangerously) stole into his storage cupboard, where we found a collection of oil portraits. Even at our unsophisticated age, we realised that they were superb. One mate, Hugo Weaving, who later became a famous actor and starred in *The Matrix* and *Lord of the Rings*, seemed to live his life on the edge the whole time at school and dared to ask Terry if he ever painted. We found out that this was how he relaxed. Years later we realised the privilege we had had of being taught by a Renaissance man of the highest order.

The most rewarding profession

I taught for about 15 years, and some of that included being a head. I only had one year as a head when I didn't teach. During those years I am really proud of the impact I know I had on my students. I admit that I didn't get it right with all of them. One set of parents asked for their child to be removed from my tutor group because I was too hard on him. I certainly erred on the high-expectations, no-excuses side of any fence that exists on the matter, and early on in my career I was too blunt in my approach. I still remember the ignominy of sitting in a room with the parents and the head, listening to the parents complaining about me. The head had warned me to keep quiet, so I wasn't able to defend myself. Agony.

Teaching is a highly nuanced, complex art, where the most effective teachers build up a range of strategies over years and years of practice. I opted out of the classroom too early to do that and moved instead into what in many ways is a less complex but equally demanding role of senior administrator, or leader, in schools. More of that later.

Louise Fenner and Louise Barnwell were in my class when I moved to my second school, in the '90s. I am including them because they put up with me and never complained about some of the challenges I gave them. They were both keen students. I was told that the class – year 8 (12-year-olds) should be stretched to the full, as the kids were high achievers. OK, I thought, why don't I start by getting them to learn Robert Browning's

'The Pied Piper of Hamelin' and to put on an outdoor performance to parents? Simples. We're talking more than 300 lines, with dialogue throughout. We did the whole thing in about three weeks. Afterwards, the parents looked at me strangely. Some, I'm convinced, thought I was a lunatic; others a genius come to rescue their children from mediocrity. Louise and Barny, as she was called, performed brilliantly, throwing themselves into the parts I had given them. Years later, at the Wellington Festival of Education, they approached me after I'd been involved in a panel discussion, to tell me that they were both now teachers and to encourage me that they had liked what I'd said in the discussion. They clearly were ambitious and wanted to deepen their teaching practice. A special moment.

Ross Brockman got in touch with me a few years ago. Now a manager at Google, he had been in my English class in years 7 and 8. He gobbled up everything I gave to him. I introduced him to zany classics such as Douglas Adams's *The Hitchhiker's Guide to the Galaxy* and got him to write sonnets. He questioned everything and did exactly as I asked. Whatever we say about 'fixed mindset' and the dangers of labelling people, Ross was phenomenally bright and eager to learn. I had the huge task of stretching him. I'm not sure how well I did, but he invited me to lunch at the Google restaurant years later. By then I was running The Key. Ross took apart my whole organisation and put it back together in front of me, analysing the sector and what our offer was, what my key metrics must be and how the quality/price coefficient must be complex. He spoke with an intensity of focus that was quite exhausting to keep up with. I was delighted that he was working in an organisation that was full of people with similar brains.

I finished one lesson teaching junior high students at the start of my teaching practice in the US to find that someone had left a big shiny apple on my desk. The kids were from poor farming families and this, I was subsequently told, was a traditional gift (going back centuries) to the teacher at the start of a new academic year. I was really taken by the gesture and by the bond that existed between families and the teacher represented by such a gift.

One child I worked with when he was about 11 seemed to be in a world of his own. He talked to himself and had a high squeaky voice. I can't remember why, but I made him sit right at the front of the class. He huffed and puffed his way through lessons and made it clear that this was not his preferred subject. His handwriting was distressing to look at. If he was asked a question, he would laugh nervously in the hope that I would give up and move on to another pupil. Once we were studying a complicated poem and I got him to explain what was going on. I wouldn't leave him alone when he began his squeaking and puffing. I simply said, 'Michael, I'm not going to let you off the hook. I know you can do this, so we'll all simply wait for you to explain.' After what felt like an age, he eventually expressed in phrases of exceptional clarity what the poet was trying to achieve. It was a moment of revelation for the class and for me. From that point on I never let him get away with anything other than exceptional work. His parents invited my wife and me out to a restaurant. I remember it because we had little money at the time and going out to a restaurant was the sort of classy activity we never indulged in. Michael's father said at the start of the meal how grateful he and his wife were that I had broken through to Michael in a way that no one else had, and that he was now a different child. I remember feeling embarrassed, and throwing off the praise by way of avoiding an emotional response. But it still strikes me how powerful a teacher can be in unlocking children in a way that reveals both to them and the world around them that they have something worthwhile in them. I can't think of another profession or role which affords this privilege. Maybe that of being a parent? But so often children discount the words of their parents, dismissing them as unfounded or simply wrong. I know my own do.

As a head I would tell teachers that they had the opportunity of seeing the differences between otherwise similar human beings. After all, children in a class are usually of a similar age and have numerous other similarities. Therefore it should be easier for a teacher to spot the smaller differences. What sort of language and phrases and idioms did different children use? Which of them went for the more sophisticated thoughts? Who challenged the way teacher questions were articulated? Which children got bored more easily? Which seemed to cope with higher levels of challenge? And so on and so on. The differences become infinite once you start looking for them. I would ask teachers to point out to children how they were different and how that difference was special. I would get them to tell the parents. After all, parents usually only have a maximum of two or three other children to compare. And it is tough to describe children on a learning journey except in relative terms to how the others are doing.

Back to an earlier point about the need for teachers to have more experience: it is too easy to describe children's learning in fairly bland terms. I know that many primary teachers have three main descriptors for how children in their class are progressing in each subject and therefore have only three different types of comment when writing reports for parents. That really is so reductive as to dismiss the significant opportunity a teacher has to notice difference, and to do so in detail. Bland, generic reporting should be binned, to my mind. Teachers should work with each other to develop much more detailed observations of children and what they are like, in the quest to discover the potential in each child. This of course needs to be done in a way that does not bury the teacher in extra work. Challenging, but possible, and potentially highly impactful.

Such a discovery would lead to figuring out precisely how children learn. I was taught languages in a highly structured way that was exceptionally challenging and rigorous. I was taught science in a formulaic (sorry) way that was slow and tedious, meaning that I quickly lost concentration. I wasn't genetically indisposed to understanding science. Both my parents were doctors, for goodness' sake. But the teacher treated us as a mass (sorry again) of pupils, rather than a gathering of individuals, and there was little attempt to ensure that every child was keeping up on the journey.

Get it right, and the teacher's role is life-transforming and endlessly exciting. Get it wrong and it is a tedious, repetitive profession full of stress and exhaustion. It's up to the senior leaders to set environments where the former is the norm. It is up to teachers to embrace the potential that they have in their hands.

Philippe Baling – the explainer

My eldest daughter was good at French and her A level teacher told her to apply for Oxford. In her interview she was taught how to make participles agree and to consider what the rules might be. Philippe Baling had made me learn this when I was 11. I still remember having drummed into me, 'The past participle conjugated with *avoir* agrees with the preceding direct object; the past participle conjugated with *être* agrees with the subject.'

The next task, of course, was to figure out what a direct object was.

I remember at the time finding it extraordinarily difficult to understand. But *Monsieur* Baling, as we called him, explained it, then tested us straightaway to check the level of our understanding. Then he explained some more. Then he tested us again. There was lots of queuing up with books and lots of very truncated conversations between teacher and individual pupils. Eventually I began to understand. We did loads of examples. Those were the days when chapters in the exercise book would have ten sentences you had to translate, in order to demonstrate your understanding.

I remember his typically French curly handwriting as he wrote on the blackboard. He was not a patient man and he and I fell out a number of times. I was somewhat scared of him. Those were the days when discipline and assault were not yet clearly understood as being quite distinct from each other, and pupils lived in a permanent state of anxiety about their safety. But, just to be clear, Monsieur never hit us. I'm just saying that the environment we lived in at school meant that it wouldn't have been altogether extraordinary to have had something thrown at us, or worse. Corporal punishment still existed in the '70s, and well into the '80s. Its application was not well codified. I don't think schools had too many policies in those days.

French lessons under Monsieur Baling were difficult. We moved from one tough concept to another. He used to get us to translate from French magazines, such as *Paris Match*. We had to research specific subjects and give talks in French. And we were only 12 or so at the time. It was extremely demanding.

Looking back, however, I am glad that the demands placed on me were so tough. I remember visiting a little primary school in the middle of Somerset a few years ago. Three things are dominant in my memory from that visit. First, they kept chickens. Second, the school council, made up of children, decided the rules by which the school was run. Third, they discovered that a theatre producer from London had a house locally and they persuaded her to write a cut-down version of a different Shakespeare play each year, using original Shakespearean language. When I visited, they had just done a 45-minute *A Midsummer Night's Dream* the week before. I challenged the head as to whether the children could even understand what they were saying and she retorted that of course it was difficult to start with, but by the end of the project pupils' understanding had grown hugely and they very much enjoyed the drama. She was convinced that placing such demands on them was one of the best things the school was doing for its children.

I read a biography of Cardinal Basil Hume, head of the Catholic Church in England during the '90s and a man I had a huge respect for, in which he said that his early years of training to become a Benedictine monk and priest nearly finished him off. He was sent to Rome for several years, where the lectures were entirely in Latin. He wrote that he would literally be in tears at the end of the day for the first couple of months until gradually the light dawned and he began to make sense of what he was hearing. In later life, he said, it had been of considerable help to him to be able so easily to understand the great works of literature in their original language, along with the canon law on which the Catholic Church depended for its organisation.

We tend to get all rather binary when we talk about giving children challenges. Monsieur Baling gave us some apparently monstrous challenges at the age of 12 that might have tested A level students, but he never chucked us in the deep end to sink or swim. I remember the endless explanations in front of the blackboard, where he would not sit down until he was satisfied that we had all understood. Then came the written tests. He would speak French to us as a reward almost, when he thought we had done enough work to enjoy listening. Yes, we struggled with what seemed such alien constructs to start with. He (along with a couple of teachers at the senior school I went onto) is responsible for my love of the French language, which would never have developed if I hadn't first understood the basic engineering of how it worked.

Many years later I found myself as head of a school in deepest Kent, where several year groups had classes following the French national curriculum. So, there were two classes in year 7, for example, which followed the English national curriculum, with a third made up of children from international French families based all over the place. These families could send their children to us without them having to return to France itself. About 30% of the teaching staff were French, including one of the two assistant heads. One year I accompanied the French exchange to Bourg-en-Bresse, near Macon, close to the border with Switzerland. When the train arrived and 50 or so children and a few staff got off to meet our French counterparts, I was immediately told that the local radio station wished to have an interview with me. I agreed, thinking that, like in England, this would be a couple of questions taking up a few minutes of air time. In the event, it took a full half-hour and I ended up using every word of the language, every idiom, every expression I had ever learnt during my education. Reflecting afterwards how I had even survived the experience, I thought back to how Monsieur Baling would have expected a fair performance and how I simply needed to give it a go.

Perversely, even today, I deliberately want to be in situations which are challenging, where I don't have any guarantee that I will be alright, which are downright tough. We know that our brains are so plastic that they learn to adapt to these new, different, demanding circumstances and, in doing so, leave a permanent change in their make-up. How else would we ever have created concert pianists able to memorise and play long concertos, interpreting them in fresh ways, or the shopkeepers in some of our cities who can speak six or seven languages in order to meet the needs of their various customers?

Teaching isn't for perfectionists

Perfection doesn't exist in teaching. It can't and it shouldn't. My wife trained to be a biology teacher over a four-year period. She did very well in her teaching practices. She got a 2:1 in her degree at a time when typically about 40% of the year group got 2:1s, 40% got 2:2s, 10% got firsts and the rest thirds or fails. She worked hard and methodically. She liked her subject, although she'd admit that she wasn't passionate about it.

After all that effort, she decided at the end of the degree not to go into teaching and ended up becoming a business analyst in a software company. I have had numerous conversations with her about this decision over the years we have been together. Her own explanation is that she could never get the students to do *exactly* what she wanted all of the time. Her lesson plans never went *totally* to plan. The kids never responded *completely* as she had prepared for them to respond. Consequently, she could never be other than anxious in her lessons, and she presumed that that would never change.

And her reasons for staying away from the classroom are in large part the reasons why I made a beeline for it. I loved the danger, the uncertainty. I relished the challenge of the kids who just didn't want to be in the room. Unlike her, I loved my subject and wanted everyone to realise the pleasure of being able to communicate clearly and crisply, and the joy of being able to feel another person's life through literature. I enjoyed the variety of the different mixes of individuals coming through the door each lesson. I liked being put to the test and having to be on my A game if I was to succeed.

Of course you can't get it right all the time for every pupil. They are all very different and some will click with you more than others. This came home to me more than ever when we were doing some staff training early on in my first headship. We had a facilitator who took us through the Myers-Briggs Type Indicator (MBTI). You take a test, or rather, you answer loads of questions which ask you to state your preference between two choices. This gives you a 'type', made up of four parts, related to how you take in information and engage with the world around you. We all took the test, came out with the four-letter descriptors, then mapped the whole staff into the 16 boxes representing the different descriptors. The shock for me was that I was the only ENTJ in the room.

The next part of the training was all about how different personalities tend to struggle with other personalities and what they need to work on in order to get on with them. This was definitely one of those wake-up moments in my life, when I was forced to realise that, of course, not everyone viewed the world in the same way I did. Now please don't think of me as a complete idiot. I know I have a tendency to be a bit naive at times, but I really went through something of an epiphany.

Not only did I start to figure out ways of getting through to colleagues on the staff and thinking about how I might better appreciate how other people behaved, but I'm convinced that my teaching started to improve because I was coming to realise that I had a multiplicity of personalities and world views and ways of communicating walking through my door every time the lesson bell rang. Some would naturally love the books and poems I wanted to study. Others would hate them. Revelation.

That explained why in my first couple of years' teaching I couldn't get through to one particular boy in my tutor group. He hardly spoke in lessons and was generally timid about the school. I was constantly giving him pep talks and telling him what he could achieve if he put his mind to it. If only I had realised that he was deeply introverted and needed space to think, that he was actually a profoundly reflective individual who was quite happy to be on his own rather than being cajoled into all the activities I was trying to push him into, I would not have alienated him in the way I did.

So, it's no wonder that teaching is so complex as to be impossible to achieve perfection as a teacher. People are hugely complex and different from each other. They learn differently. The most successful teachers get that, and adjust their teaching accordingly. You might have come across various pretty simplistic models that come by from time to time to address this. One of the most popular in recent times has been VAK, where students have 'learning preferences'. It wasn't so long ago that some schools insisted that teachers mark in their registers a 'V', an 'A' or a 'K' against the name of each of their students to show whether they considered them to be a visual, auditory or kinaesthetic learner. You can make your diagnosis, apparently, by giving a child a problem to think about, then watch their eyes to see if they go upwards (definitely visual), straight (auditory for sure) or to the ground (a kinaesthetic without a toots of a doubt). Quite why we have such a tendency to jump on bandwagons in teaching, I don't fully understand, but we clearly do. I guess you can't really be an outstanding teacher if you don't engage in psychology of some sort, probably whether you realise it or not, because so much of the job is about trying to understand how to engage a class of different individuals. How do they think? How can I get them interested, so that they might even want to learn? What prejudices do they already hold about my subject and how can I rectify these?

As a teacher, my approach bordered on the edge of lunacy. The only way I managed to teach one class when to use an apostrophe with 'its' was by getting them to do what we called the 'apostrophe dance', which involved a hop which was quite difficult.

> You only (right foot down) use (left) an apos (right) tro-phe (left) with its (right) when it's (jump up in the air and do an about-turn) *it is* (both feet slammed into the floor).

Come on, live a little. It worked, and that's all that mattered. The other thing that used to bug me as a teacher is that the lessons used only to be about 40 minutes each and kids would race over from a science lab or wherever they had been prior to my lesson. How dare they not be totally prepared and zen-like in readiness for my pearls of wisdom! I had to switch them into the appropriate mode as quickly as possible. I tried getting one person in each class to be the 'two-minute monitor'. They all had to put their heads on the desks and keep total silence until the monitor released them. That worked for a bit, but was difficult to keep going. To address another frustration, I introduced a 'jabber monitor', who made us open our jabber books (I had one, too) and write continuously for the allotted time, without stopping at all, about anything at all. Did it work? Hmm. Not sure, but I think it may have got some kids over the fear of putting pen to paper.

My younger brother saw the list of teachers I planned to include in this book and questioned why I thought one teacher in particular had been effective. He had found the person in question boring and machine-like in the way they had taught. At university I had a lecturer on Dickens whom I found completely inspiring and led me to understand the author in ways I hadn't expected. Other students couldn't wait to move onto a different module to escape the boredom. Why such a completely different take on the same individual?

It's impossible to be perfect as a teacher, but I guess you can mix up your styles so that you appeal to the multiplicity of personalities and learning preferences you have in front of you. I loved history as a subject but was always floored when the teacher at the end of the course would simply tell us to 'go and learn it'. Only years later did I come to realise that I am a big-picture person who needs to see things as a whole. If only my teachers had realised that and helped me to revise in a way appropriate to that. At school I wrote pages and pages of notes from the notes I'd already taken, while for my university finals, and exams done since, I have used A3 poster cards to encapsulate all my thinking about a particular play or theme or whatever.

An effective teacher can't afford to be too set on particular methods of teaching, especially if they are a bit one-dimensional. The nearest you'll get to any notion of perfection is to be multi-dimensional in your approach.

GTH

We were fascinated by Mr Humby. To us eight-year-olds, he was a giant. I mean literally, not figuratively. He had to stoop to get into our pre-fab classroom. I'm guessing six foot six or so. And sooo old. Big thick-framed glasses with eager, piercing eyes made bigger by the lenses. I have the impression he might once have been in the military. Navy perhaps. Or maybe that's just my memory of the pipe he always carried translating itself too presumptuously into my consciousness. Almost from the minute you met him, you knew you were in the presence of authority and you rarely forgot. If you *did*, it wasn't for long: his deep voice was quick to check any behaviour that was in any way off-piste.

But he was a warm character, very caring and quick to spot when you weren't happy. He would put a huge hand on your shoulder and express just the right level of sympathy for whatever you'd been through.

He was eccentric. He didn't tick correct answers in your book, he put his initials after the answer. GTH, with the curve of the G pulled forward like an elongated spinnaker in a strong wind. I assume George, or Gordon, then Terence and, of course, Humby, which softened the overall impression. How perfectly a name can fit how a character asserts itself.

Everything in Mr Humby's lessons was ritualised. We would work on our grammar on a Monday, because 'As Englishmen', (it was a boys-only school in those days) we had to know how to use the Queen's English to perfection. We would do endless exercises designed to embed our understanding of subject and object and verb and pronoun and synonym and homonym and whatever the next thing was. But on Fridays, GTH would always read to us from *The Island of the Blue Dolphins* or *Treasure Island* or *Tom Sawyer* and his dramatic rendition would hold us spellbound to the extent that we would implore him to carry on after the bell had gone.

Looking back, I learned more in the couple of years that Mr Humby taught me than I did from most other teachers I can remember. He drilled us hard, but rewarded us with encouragement. Getting praise from him was worth more than from most teachers, because he didn't hand it out too generously. He was a tough marker: nothing but the very best would earn top grades from him. If you got anything wrong, he explained it, rather impatiently as I recall, and you had to do it again until you got it right. It made me slow down a bit (I always wanted to be the first to finish) and check my work more carefully before handing it over.

He was my English teacher the following year. I remember having to learn a whole poem by John Masefield. 'Sea Fever'. I remember it still: 'I must go down to the seas again, to the lonely sea and the sky...' He drilled into us how carefully the poet had chosen each and every word and how, therefore, we dishonoured the poet if we made up our own version. I now realise how much I copied from teachers like Mr Humby in my own teaching. I would explain to my own students why it was so important to read the exact words that an author has written and how arrogant it would be to assume we can use our own instead. To fail to get the words exactly right, when memorising the poem, meant that we weren't getting the exact sense of what the poet intended. I always remembered that when studying Shakespeare years later at university.

One of the other things that has stuck with me over time is the need to use words precisely, when the context requires it. He made you look at sentences and figure out what each word was doing. If you swapped two words around, how did that change the sense? He challenged the use of pedestrian words and insisted you always look for the precise word, 'in this finest and richest of languages, the Queen's English', in order to express precisely what you wanted to convey.

So, maybe there was a bit of pomp, a bit of melodrama, even a slightly superior air about a GTH lesson, but 'By George', you were going to learn the material he put before you. We were in no doubt about that. There was a job to do. It was an incredibly important job. GTH was going to do the job well. There was a toughness about him, an underlying rigour that made it clear he wasn't messing about. It wasn't entertainment, however much we enjoyed such a lot of the learning matter. It was fundamental to our development as educated people. I am hugely grateful to him for what he inculcated in me.

Rubbish teaching

I didn't go to lessons to be entertained. I wanted to learn. I have sharp memories of four particular teachers who took me backwards in the subject they taught. I'm not being dramatic here; I'm deadly serious. I've agreed with the publisher not to name them, as I don't think they want to deal with any subsequent lawsuits. And neither do I.

The first was a Latin teacher who taught me Cambridge Latin – a different kind of approach which took you straight into the literature without worrying too much about learning the grammar first. He was one of the kindest, gentlest people I came across in the teaching profession, but I never felt I was making progress and I found myself getting angrier and angrier as the weeks and months went by. It wasn't the subject per se that frustrated me. I had loved the sense of achievement I had experienced from previous Latin teachers. Mr D taught me ancient history as well for two years leading up to O level. The only two Cs I got (my lowest passes) were in his two subjects. I just couldn't engage with the subject properly. It was painfully slow – and I wanted to go at pace. I couldn't see the point of what I was learning. I didn't have any sense of achievement. In the end I put it down to being stupid. I now know that I wasn't stupid; the teacher was just incompetent. I am angry even today, because I realise how common a scenario this is. Children write themselves off as thick because an incompetent teacher allows them to do so. Headteachers should be ruthless in dealing with situations like this. They are hugely dangerous.

Mr F was always keen to make maths fun. We played game after game. He would tell us jokes and have a lot of banter. He loved to use language that would make him popular with the 15-year-old students he taught. I started my time with him feeling reasonably competent in the subject. After two years, I begged the school to let me move down a set, where I ended up with the brilliant, if unexciting, Mr Wood, who would not allow any of his students to fail. Mr F didn't know the extent of my misunderstanding of various concepts. In maths, of course, if you misunderstand one element of the subject, it often means you can't understand the next bit either. His reports to my parents told them that I struggled with the subject. He was bang on. I did. Why? Because I couldn't understand what he wanted from me. I was a serious, rather diffident individual at that age and I couldn't figure out a lot of how an adult's humour worked. Others laughed at me because I didn't understand his quips and sarcastic remarks. I felt humiliated, so I withdrew, accepting my stupidity. The doors of my brain started closing towards maths.

I bombed at science at school. My parents were both doctors. My mother was an anaesthetist. You would have thought that there would have been some kind of inherited ability in the subject. But for two years, from 11 to 13, I loathed the teacher who taught me and dreaded the lessons. Mr G. He teased me in front of the other kids, calling me 'Fairy' in front of other children, because he felt I had missed a couple of tackles in rugby. I felt belittled and permanently angry in his classes. And the way I got back at him was by making no effort and showing no enthusiasm whatsoever.

What an idiot I was, but then I was only young. Why was someone like that responsible for teaching such an important subject? Each week he'd come in and decide there and then what we were going to do. 'Right. When did we last do chromatography? OK – let's do that.' No effort to get us excited as to what we might be able to discover via chromatography. We just went through the motions and wrote the notes, which I don't remember him even looking at. This is not just unfortunate or a pity. It is unforgiveable. I was at such an impressionable age and I could have done so well, with the right approach. Why did the head of the school allow this situation? It is simply inexcusable. *Reverse teaching* – in other words, teaching that is so bad that it sends a child backwards – should be treated as a nasty tumour in a school. It either needs to be given very powerful medicine, or it needs to be cut out altogether.

Then, at 13, we were taught the sciences separately. By that stage I had the firm view that science was not my thing. So I wasn't well disposed to any of the teachers. But my chemistry teacher, Mrs C, was truly awful. She had a high-pitched voice and screamed at us regularly. She would shout at the whole class, despite the fact that only two or three kids would be misbehaving. Her first lessons were all about cooking, and the comparison to chemistry. That did absolutely zilch to engage me in the subject. My enthusiasm for chemistry, biology and physics never recovered. And I'm still a bit angry, even now. If only those teachers had refused to allow me to bow out in the way I had done, I am convinced I would have committed to working. But I, like countless others, simply blamed myself for creating my own problem. Wrong, wrong, wrong. Those teachers could have sorted me, but they didn't. How dare Mr G humiliate me as he did, killing my attitude to the subject which was potentially so exciting? Why did the head of that school not realise what was going on, and do something about it? Why should any teacher get away with behaving in such a way?

We really have to sort this out, as I'm only too aware that reverse teaching is still commonplace. Kids would be better off in classes of a hundred with a superb teacher, than in a class of ten with a reverse teacher. Allowing such teaching to continue damages the profession's reputation and repels new entrants to it. A friend of mine used to teach at Guildford High School, one of the most successful schools in the country when it comes to exam results. The teachers, my friend claimed, were competitive with each other, all of them wanting to prove how effective they were. Well, you know what, I don't have a big problem with that. It might not be ideal; in fact it might at times make for a toxic atmosphere in the staff room. But if the children gain from it, then fine. Teaching is a finely balanced activity, the practitioner having to nuance their approach delicately. We should ensure that the world sees this, and comes to delight in and reward effective teaching appropriately. Let us hope that the College of Teaching makes its mark, and a profession which has such potential to change lives owns its impact a bit more and starts to assert itself more effectively on the public stage.

There's nothing wrong with boring

One thing I can't explain is why I loved my Shakespeare and Dickens lecturer at university, but so many other students didn't. They found Dr Russell boring. To me, he was a wonderful man, an oracle of knowledge, endlessly open to taking my questions, someone who gave me such helpful feedback on the many essays I submitted. He saw links between themes, he drew similarities between characters across different literary periods. I loved the fact that he was such an expert. He had, I believe, done his PhD on Dickens and had written a number of influential papers about the writer. I guess I was in awe for much of the time.

But he would, I admit, sit at the front of the lecture room and talk from his handwritten detailed notes while smoking one of his Hamlet cigars. Maybe not everyone found it easy to engage.

I think the opposite of what happened to me in science happened to me in other subjects. I was given enough confidence in English, in languages, in history, that I was well able to master the subject. So maybe I didn't need the subsequent teachers to be of the same calibre? Maybe I had enough built-in confidence in those subjects for me not to wilt when I had a teacher who didn't have the same talent.

Except that I think Mike Russell *was* talented. He was, for one thing, endlessly patient and never got riled if a student asked him a question that showed ignorance. Because he loved his subject matter so deeply, he didn't mind hanging around with students who were still in the starting blocks if he thought he might get them into the race itself, a race which he knew had great significance.

Somehow I got the sense from Mike that Dickens demonstrated such a deep understanding of human life through his novels that the sensitive reader could only be greatly enriched in the process. That thought set me off on a voyage of discovery, where I was keen to reach the next stage. Each lecture, I became more and more fascinated. How did Dickens weave climactic metaphor into his narrative to increase the tension? Brilliant. Do the characters of Amy Dorrit and Dora Spenlow show that Dickens had an idealised and rather hollow view of women? Can a feminist like Dickens? Contrast the portrayal of women in Dickens with that of the Brontë sisters. The discussions got more and more interesting as we engaged with more and more of the detail. My mind would come alive in these sessions.

Mike didn't stage-manage his lectures in the way others did. He didn't vary his presentation much, but he drew (most of) us into the subject matter and got us to think. Interesting: my eldest daughter did English A level and told me about one of her teachers who had an encyclopaedic knowledge of 20th century literature and a phenomenal ability to relate themes and characters in one book, or from one author, to that of others. She said that some students complained that he simply sat there and spoke at them. But *she* found him inspiring and fascinating. Perhaps there is something genetic going on here!

This teacher's head, who was a friend of mine, told me in confidence that the teacher always caused concern: he simply failed to live up to most of the teaching standards expected of the profession. But, said my friend, he manages to get good results, and a healthy number of his students go on to read the subject at university. Once again, it is dangerous to dismiss (sometimes literally) teachers when they don't fit the norms that are in vogue at a particular point in time.

Of course, the title of this chapter is designed to shock, and not really be taken literally. Much of learning grammar and vocabulary is pretty tedious, but it doesn't have to be repellent to the learner. If, as the teacher, you can show that once these are learned, you can put them to good use straightaway, then the tedium becomes a means to an end. Think of trainee doctors who have to slave through anatomy books, learning the nerve systems of the wrist. Pretty unappealing. But start showing videos of operations that have repaired parts of these systems through complex surgery, hearing the surgeons referring to the different terms that you have been learning, and the whole exercise seems to have more point to it. Get kids to learn material through hours of dull concentration without then showing them how to apply this learning, and you're just being cruel.

An observer standing outside the window into the lecture room simply watching the body language of people in the lecture might be forgiven for assuming the subject matter was boring. But surely the mind can be animated without a demonstration of physical exertion? Well, I'm sure that's the case for many students. I guess what would have drawn in the other students would have been some effort to encourage group discussion, presentations from students, paired work. The trick would have been not to lose the invitation from Mike to walk with him into the Aladdin's cave of his knowledge and understanding of the subject. Once again we realise that masterful teaching is where these apparent tensions are subtly reconciled. How can a teacher stay on the journey of discovery themselves, pass on their knowledge and their passion for their subject to the students, while engaging them thoroughly throughout the process of doing so?

I guess the answer is to keep trying for years and years until you get better and better at it. But getting it right must be like finding gold. No one expects it to be an easy task, but it's worth the effort.

Brian Keating – the extender

Some teachers have a significant, long-lasting impact on their students. I was only taught by Brian Keating for one year, but he made a huge impression on me. He got me to realise that I was, in fact, really capable at French. I remember his lessons for the amount that happened in them: they were exhausting. You prepared hard beforehand – there was usually some kind of test at the start of each one – and you hoped that whatever work you had submitted had been thought good enough by Brian. You certainly knew about it if it hadn't. He was quite happy to lecture you in front of your peers and make you feel you had not just let yourself down, but everyone else as well.

It was definitely not comfortable being a 14-year-old in Brian's classes. Well, it wasn't comfortable for anyone. He always struck me as a fairly isolated fellow. He was pretty acerbic in his language and there was a sharp edge to many of his comments. This led to him having a major falling out with the 17- and 18-year-olds in the cricket team first XI in his role as coach. I can't remember if he ended up standing down from that role, but it created major drama in the school at the time. He avoided playing safe, did Brian. He told it as he saw it. He wasn't the cover-'em-with-praise-and-they'll-come-along-with-you kind of teacher. A Lancastrian, and proud of it, he told you directly what he thought of you. I guess I just wanted to get better and better and, because I saw myself doing so, through tests and marks, and of course, by comparing my results to those of my classmates, I knew he was having a positive impact on my work.

During my time running The Key, I have visited scores of different schools: primary, secondary, special, independent, all-through, academy, maintained, whatever. I have noticed that independent schools in general are more relaxed about giving their teachers more latitude in how they behave towards students. At least, there seems to be more tolerance of eccentricity. Brian Keating was not an easy character and he would face a string of complaints from some of the schools I know today. But I still maintain that there was something quite masterful about his approach. What I'm coming to realise while writing this book is that most brilliant teachers are far from being completely rounded, perfect individuals. And I suppose my point is that we shouldn't even try. You don't need to be perfect in order to be a brilliant teacher. If you keep trying, you're going to fail. And then you'll leave. And that is disastrous for the kids whose lives you were going to change. So, don't even try. Just be yourself. Authenticity is worth a lot.

I remember often being on my feet during Brian's lessons. We went systematically through all the tenses and were forever having quizzes and competitions where you stood until you were 'out'. He managed our competitive streaks well and we enjoyed the challenge. I compared what my daughter was doing in her A level studies with what we had done with Brian. We were pushed and pushed way ahead of where my daughter was, when we were three years younger. He expected us to cope. More than that: thrive.

Gold miners get to discover something amazing, when they eventually find what they are looking for. But there is back-breaking hard work to be done before they do so. Brian worked exceptionally hard on our behalf. He decided we were going to learn the phonetic sign system from one of the most advanced dictionaries at the time, for example, and he taught us to pronounce every single symbol. Once we had done so, he never again allowed us to make the most minor of errors – between *lait* and *les*, for example, or *c'est* and *ses* – in the way we pronounced words. And I never forgot, afterwards. He just drove it home and went over and over it again. I just don't see the same attention to detail as being commonplace in the teaching I see today. But it should be.

Looking after teachers

Teachers are a weird combination of professional technicians and vulnerable artists. They need looking after. The best heads I know have always figured out ways of doing this. Professor Pat Preedy, when she ran an infant and junior school in Solihull, came up with a scheme where teachers could bring their laundry to school and it would be washed and ironed for a small charge. A prep school in Folkestone I came across offered chiropody for its staff every month. Sir Andrew Carter, at South Farnham School, will not allow teachers to bring work into the staff room: auxiliary staff make the coffee for them at breaktime, and wash up afterwards. If teachers need to come to a parents consultation in the evening, they will be served (at the school's expense) supper beforehand. The role of teaching assistant is to enable the teacher to focus solely on the highest-value activity.

Teachers are extraordinary if you enable them to be, Sir Andrew argues. They are difficult to recruit, take time to reach their best, are often a bit prickly (any head would agree) and deserve maximum support. They can be ridiculously sensitive, like actors. Their jobs are tough and they put their souls on the line in front of their charges. They need huge energy to play a role in front of large groups of people. They need support, rest and recognition. They need to know that their work has been recognised and appreciated. Heads and deputies should go round the school each day noticing the work that is being done and giving their encouragement. A research study carried out in 2014/15 by the teacher recruitment organisation Teach First found that the biggest reason their graduates wanted to leave teaching was a lack of recognition by senior management. They found that teachers saw huge significance in the head or deputy coming around each day and spending 30 seconds asking them how they were getting on. Should we be surprised?

When your work is intense and exhausting, you need to see its impact. If you've been on stage for two hours, the audience engagement and applause is not just appreciated; it's needed. The same is true for teachers. If they have the kind of headteacher who won't come out of their office, and rarely gives them any thanks, they wilt. It's not that they are excessively fragile; they are simply human. In our efforts to recognise the professional role of the teacher, we can mask the fact that it is a fundamentally human activity that also needs to be seen and treated as such. Effort from the teacher, plus encouragement and recognition from the head, has a multiplying impact on the teacher's efficacy.

But teachers are highly trained, highly skilled professionals. They should not be treated as fast-food workers in a high-street franchise. I have big problems with 'teacher of the year', 'teacher of the month' and suchlike, which address teaching in an overly reductive way. The work of a teacher is achieved over a long timeframe. That's why observations of 20-minute sections of lessons by school inspectors were never likely to be a sufficiently valid means of assessing a teacher's efficacy.

I remember, as a head, telling parents that one of the most effective ways of helping their children's teachers to do a good job was by giving them positive feedback and encouragement. In one parent–teacher meeting that I had with one of my daughter's A level teachers, I told the teacher how much my daughter respected him and wanted to work hard for him. I told him how hugely grateful we were to him for what he was doing for her. He was someone who worked incredibly hard for his students and expected a lot from them in return. He seemed the perfect professional to me. But when I thanked him and told him how much he was appreciated, he found it difficult to hide his emotion. I could see how much he was moved by (what I thought was) such a small token of appreciation.

Mrs Hardwick – do your corrections

Brigid Hardwick was a doll-like lady, who can't have been more than five feet tall. She was always immaculately turned out and had amazing italic handwriting. Her accent made her sound like a cousin of the Queen. She was almost always positive, she loved teaching French, particularly French literature, and she couldn't have been more encouraging. Her voice was high pitched and rather shrill. To the group of adolescent boys in my class, she was something of an enigma. We simply didn't know how to react to her. We were very mean to her at times, but she went along with it. The class had a sort of platform or dais at the front, for the teacher's desk and chair. For our weekly test, we would have put up posters on the front of the desk (on the teacher's blind side) with all the vocabulary or grammar we had to learn. She was delighted with our results.

At one time there seemed to be a kitten out on the windowsill, or at least, kitten-like noises were definitely coming from somewhere around the window. Of course, the delicate, animal-loving sensitivities of a class of 15-year-old hairy, smelly adolescents meant that we had to drop everything and rush over to the window to ensure that none of God's creatures was possibly in harm's way. And then, suddenly, the kitten seemed to have moved over to the other side of the room. Or, at least, the noise had.

Mimicking animal noises was one of the talents I had developed at the time.

I think, in retrospect, that Brigid went along with the teenage humour. She didn't let it get her annoyed. It was a mild diversion in an otherwise industrious lesson. She wanted to be collaborative in her approach. She taught me again for A level, when the class vetoed our study of *Journal d'un Curé de Campagne* by Georges Bernanos. For goodness' sake, it was about 300 pages long. We wanted to do *Candide* by Voltaire instead, which we knew to be only 100 pages, and full of filth. Brigid expressed her disappointment, but the following week we exchanged our country priest books for the porn. We loved all the innuendo in the book. But we loved even more the way Brigid pretended to have no idea what it meant.

We did lots of exercises in our books, to demonstrate our understanding of the grammar we were learning. Brigid made us spend forever going through them, making corrections and proving to her that we had understood where we had gone wrong and had made amends. She would walk around the room until she had seen everyone's work. This was tedious, I have to admit, but highly effective. I was pretty good at the subject and tended to get most of the exercises correct, so Brigid immediately gave me the most stingingly difficult additional exercises, where I had to use three pronouns in a sentence, with two before the verb and one afterward, where the past participle had to agree precisely. I loved these challenges and enjoyed her 'Yes' when I got them right.

She was one of the most passionate teachers I came across. She taught us Racine's *Phèdre* for A level. The text looked as boring a piece of literature as you could possibly imagine, but Brigid's enthusiasm would wear down the most intransigent opposition and we ended up fully engaging.

I fell out with her once, because I was a diffident teenager who at the age of 14/15 hadn't grown in comparison to my peers. I was always trying to impress them or make them laugh. In a piece of free writing we did, I tried to translate something quite obscene into rough French. On the *up* side, I think I managed pretty well (this was long before Google Translate) to do the job. On the other, Brigid felt I was being very rude and she reported me to my tutor, who gave me a real dressing down. She also wrote a fairly critical comment to my parents in my end of term report, which was depressing in one of the few subjects where my marks were actually pretty good. In fact, I think she could have given me a bit more slack and realised that I was simply lacking maturity and had been trying to impress. Not that I'm still bitter in any way, you understand.

Still, I look back on Brigid Hardwick as one of the teachers for whom I had most respect. She loved her subject, she was endlessly enthusiastic, and she refused to let anyone think the language was beyond them. French was a tough gig, full of complex rules and grammar very different from that of our own language. It was particularly technical and you had to know where to find all the information you needed if you were to succeed. It would have been so easy to 'lose' a class, but Brigid managed to keep hold of us. Everyone passed the exam with a decent grade at the end of that year, apart from one student, who re-took and did so the following term.

Teacher fragility

In my very first year as a teacher I received a stinging letter from the head, who was upbraiding me for my unprofessional behaviour towards the other team's referee in two of my team's matches. He said that I was damaging the reputation of the school and letting myself down. He told me he expected changes.

I've found the letter, carefully filed for reference, in case I get too full of myself and need to be reminded how I got things so wrong at times:

Criticism of the referee and what was interpreted as sheer bad manners caused not only an 'atmosphere' to develop, but letters of complaint to reach me from the respective heads. Our reputation has been severely tarnished and the happy, respectful relationships that we have enjoyed with the schools in question have been damaged. That this saddens and disappoints me must be the understatement of the year. You must realise that any incidents like this tend to be remembered for far too long by the school concerned. Exaggeration and embellishment take place and before anybody knows it, we can be widely labelled as an unsporting, ill-mannered and unwelcome school.

Please see that your conduct at home or away is beyond reproach and that in future there are never any more causes for the minutest complaint. Thank you.

I remember being really stung by that. For goodness' sake, I worked at least as hard as anyone else, was giving the job my all, and one of the referees (who was also his team's coach) was well known on the circuit for being a cheat. Aaagh.

It took me a good couple of days before I stopped feeling angry. I remember drafting a sharp response. I didn't even tell my wife for a day or two. Eventually I came to terms with it and wrote back to the head assuring him that I had learned my lesson and would behave differently in future. He was pleased with my response, and we moved on. On reflection, the head dealt with me superbly well. He gave me a proverbial kick up the backside and told me to change.

Very sadly, I recently became aware of a young teacher who was not so fortunate in the way his head treated him. In his first term as a secondary school English teacher, he was emailed in the evening by one of his female students asking him to explain certain words and phrases with sexual connotations in a piece of literature they were studying. Incredibly naively, he replied, explaining in full. The email correspondence continued during the evening until it was quite late. He then realised that he had been a bit too forthcoming and asked the student to delete the emails. The previous year he had achieved nothing but outstanding grades in his PGCE teaching qualification and had been told only in recent weeks how well he was doing by his head of department. The school sacked him for gross misconduct and then tried to get him barred from teaching. He has since decided never to go near teaching again, even though the government body responsible for teacher discipline did not see it as necessary to bar or restrict him in any way.

Teachers need to behave impeccably, according to the highest standards of public office. Yes, of course. But they are human beings and they need to be steered. This is particularly the case in the UK at the moment, where half the teachers in the country have less than ten years' experience. Don't misunderstand me, we have to protect children, but we also have to protect teachers. If we don't, is it any wonder that we have such problems attracting people into a profession which should be seen as the most creative and most impactful of all?

Most successful heads I know have got stories of how they have had to deal with difficult teachers. Goodness knows, I have enough stories of my own. A very talented, but rather impatient and gruff teacher was on lunch duty in a school that I ran, and was frustrated that one of our more challenging pupils was not passing up the plates in the dining room. He tapped the 12-year-old child on the side of his arm and told him to hurry up and pass the plates down. The following morning the child's parents demanded to see me first thing and complained that their child had been assaulted. I asked them what they wanted, by way of outcome. They felt that the teacher in question had never liked their child and they wanted an apology from him. I sought out the teacher and told him that, if he valued continuing with his chosen career, he needed to give a full apology to the child and his parents and explain that he had had no intention whatsoever of hurting the child. Even though he was a very proud man, he came into my room where the parents and child were sitting and could not have done a better job in grovelling. He realised he had got it wrong. But the guy was a brilliant teacher and standards in his subject were better than you'd find in most other schools. I badly did not want to lose him, but I also saw that his behaviour had been unprofessional and inexcusable. I followed this up with a letter explaining my expectations for the future. I, of course, modelled that letter on the one I had once received myself. Oh, the irony.

Why hadn't the head in the school of the young English teacher I mentioned been more subtle in the treatment he meted out? From what I heard, the teacher was very talented and liked by his students. But because of the head's extreme action, the hundred-or-so students that the teacher was responsible for were permanently deprived of his teaching, half-way through their year. Surely you only fire someone if there aren't any other reasonable options? Some of the stories I hear of dubious decision-making from headteachers are hugely upsetting. It really makes me quite mad. Talent needs to be crafted, shaped, encouraged, occasionally hammered, before it turns into the richest material. We won't get the teachers and the teaching we want and need unless we have the right leadership.

And I'm still feeling mad.

Mrs Clayton... scary

I tremble even now to remember the stern look of Mrs Clayton, my teacher in year 2. She could control a class of high-energy seven-year-olds with a slight raise of her eyebrow. She was painfully hard to please. I struggled and struggled to be awarded a gold star for a piece of work I turned in, and week after week I received encouragement but no star. It was my introduction to how cruel the world could be. Only when my aunt, Deidre, who was a teacher and was visiting us for a couple of weeks, made me spend more time and effort on my homework did I eventually manage to achieve the great prize.

For Mrs Clayton, it was all about intense focus and effort. She demanded high levels of attention. She would explain what she wanted us to do. Then she would summarise her explanation. Then she would demand that we explained it back to her. Then she expected us to work exactly to the specifications she had given us. Anything off the mark was simply not to be tolerated. If she ever raised her voice, even slightly, you knew that the great apocalypse was nigh.

Once she caught me teasing one of the girls in the class. I can't remember quite how heinous an act I had performed, but I assume it was significant. Mrs Clayton told me to come to the front of the class. She told me to think about what I had done and how ashamed I should be. She made me go back to my seat and the whole class was told to wait in silence while she left the room. Five minutes later she returned and told me I would spend the rest of the day in the class below. No greater depths of humiliation could be reached. She said I was to walk down to Mrs George's class and knock on the door.

Now this meant having to walk all the way down two long, wide, dark corridors in what was a Victorian convent, full of statues and smelling of the (over-)boiled vegetables coming from the kitchens. It was doubly terrifying because you might meet a nun on the way. Not the smiling, brightly dressed individual you might meet today, but someone in a head-to-tail dark habit who, to a seven-year-old looked like a mysterious alien from *Doctor Who*. Even now I can remember how miserable I felt and how I never ever teased a girl afterwards.

An act of extreme cruelty? Well, it was pretty tough for one of such delicate years, but it worked and it didn't involve violence or intimidation. I think. We can judge it by today's standards and call it unnecessary or humiliating, but it didn't stand out from the culture of the day as anything like that.

The school seemed to produce teachers like Mrs Clayton. They never ever had behaviour problems, despite the classes, to my recollection, being pretty huge. Teachers were very clear in what they wanted. They would not tolerate anything other than perfect manners. They expected good work. And, for the most part, they did well out of their pupils.

The best teachers are unreasonably demanding

I can think of loads and loads of examples of where teachers have been ridiculously and *unreasonably* demanding. 'Children are elastic: they stretch according to how far they are pulled' is how, I assume, such teachers think. The newly qualified year 2 teacher at my daughter's school decided that one of the best ways for children to understand what it was like to live during World War I would be to learn what felt like the entire repertoire of music hall songs that were popular at the time. My daughter was six. She's now in her twenties. Ask her to give you the lyrics to 'Danny Boy', 'It's a Long Way to Tipperary' or about ten other songs and she'll still reel them off. The amount of effort she (and we) put into it at the time was huge, but she never questioned the teacher's right to ask.

So what? Is it cruel? A friend of mine runs a programme for disaffected youngsters called 'Unlock', where a dozen children from year 9 are 'selected' in a way which prevents them from figuring out why they have been selected. They are taken to visit inspirational people and have to bring what they have learned back to share with their year group. In order to do the latter, they are taught to speak confidently in public. My friend relates how a child with whom they had worked really hard was just about to go forward to speak when her teaching assistant told her that she didn't have to do it if she didn't want to. Of course the girl then opted out, and a huge amount of work and progress was immediately lost.

If I let my own children do merely what they want, or feel comfortable, to do, they will choose the easiest path for the most part. It's human nature. The whole child-centric philosophy has been perverted over the years by many adults, reducing it to letting children do whatever they want to do.

One of the schools where I taught had what were known as the Dutch gardens. They formed an amphitheatre. For many years, before I ever got there, a Shakespeare play had been performed by 12- and 13-year-olds. I asked if the language had been simplified. Absolutely not, was the shaming response: don't be pathetic. The primary school in Somerset that I mentioned earlier in the book had been equally demanding: every child in years 5 and 6 (9- to 11-year-olds) was expected to take part. All the parents turned up and the whole enterprise was thoroughly entertaining and enjoyable. Baffle away: how is this possible? Children have no idea what their limits are. These are set by the significant adults in their lives. Set the bar wherever you like. Children will assume that what you are asking is reasonable, however it looks to other adults.

I already mentioned that I made my year 8s learn the whole of 'The Pied Piper of Hamelin': chicken feed compared to *A Midsummer Night's Dream*. Think of the Olympics and of how gymnasts in their early teens dominate the medal tables. How did they ever get there if they didn't have teachers and trainers who made them believe that they could perform to such high standards?

So many teachers make the fundamental error of assuming they are being kind to children by not demanding too much of them. Having worked in many different types of school, I would have to say that this is generally less prevalent a syndrome in independent schools, although (as a huge generalisation, I admit) it is tempting in those schools for teachers to get scared of what parents will say if they push their offspring too hard. We can so easily think that children from disadvantaged backgrounds must be incapable of understanding in the way children from more privileged backgrounds can understand. We think we are being sophisticated and reasonable in our approach, but we are actively damaging children when we adopt that approach. If I went back into the classroom now – and who knows, I might – I would push my expectations through the roof. If I went back to headship, I would work extensively with teachers to remove the limits of their expectations. I am full of self-criticism for the fact that I was far too tolerant of a 'there, there' attitude from teachers I worked with.

And look at how we have inflated our grading systems. In some universities in the UK, 25% of students are getting first-class degrees. At A level, A grades abound, in a way they never used to.

The task of any school is to create a culture where children are stretched to achieve the highest standards of learning. Teachers in that context end up resetting the whole development framework for children. Andrew Carter (sorry, *Sir* Andrew Carter) at South Farnham Academies Trust simply will not allow children to fall behind. He has a big (for a primary) school, so there might be four classes in a year group, plus a keep-up class (not sure what he actually calls it, but it's about *keeping up* rather than *catching up*). About a dozen children who are in danger of falling behind are put into a separate class and taught by the most effective teacher, whose role is to make sure their charges keep up with the rest of the year group. Once the child is back on an even keel, so to speak, they will be reintegrated back into their original class. The net effect is that it is extremely rare for a child to fail to meet the expected attainment levels for their age group. Other educationalists turn up their noses at this and call the approach factory-line-ish, or teaching by numbers. I think this is grossly unfair. Children have a right to be taught effectively and not to be left behind. We must do all we can to make absolutely sure that this is the case. The main ingredient in all of this is teacher expectation.

One of the most controversial schools in the country is a free school in West London called Michaela, named after an inspirational teacher and led by Katherine Birbalsingh. It is renowned for the classical curriculum it embraces, for getting children to memorise important texts, for learning by rote. Lunchtime conversations are deliberately structured and all children expected to contribute, while behaving impeccably. The staff are unapologetic in what they expect from students and are ambitious for getting large numbers into top universities.

Of course, to be able to push children to greater depths of learning, teachers need to be very confident of their subject matter. And they need to constantly be learning, themselves, pushing their own understanding of their subject/s deeper and deeper. So they must push *themselves* as they push their students. Schools need to ensure that teachers' professional development is part and parcel of a working week. It can't be something that only ever gets considered for two or three days a year. Teachers are experts in the art of learning. They need to keep practising that art. They need to be pushed unreasonably. Of course.

Colin Hall – the teacher of teachers

Colin Hall started his first day as head of Holland Park comprehensive school wondering what the formal meeting taking place in a side room as he entered the school was all about. He was told that it was the union representatives interviewing for the new head of English position. Just to make that clear, the teacher union was deciding who should be appointed to a leading management position. Standards at the school were poor and the place was a mess. Today, it is one of the best-looking, best-run schools in the country. Teaching is its core. I know that sounds like a fairly obvious statement, but in this school, it really is all about teaching.

Colin, the first to admit that he is an eccentric, more-than-slightly unusual individual, leads a school with a team of people who are totally dedicated to outstanding teaching. He himself takes master classes, where he gets the staff to watch him teach. I know you might think that sounds a bit arrogant, but hold that thinking. He is a brilliant teacher. He loves his subject, English literature, and has soaked the school in literature. As you walk around, there are beautifully produced quotations from major works on the walls. The annual main production is worthy of the West End. The staff show, which might be a Shakespeare play, is treated with a level of seriousness and professionalism rarely seen elsewhere. I followed him into a lesson not that long ago. A Latin lesson. Now you have to know that half the kids in the school, at least, are from very deprived backgrounds. We are not talking Eton. The teacher told him that the students had not been behaving as well as they should. Colin gave them a piercing lecture on how privileged they were to be learning the subject and how they should be proud of the fact that their teacher had studied at Oxford University. He told the teacher to let him have a report of how the next lesson had gone and that he wanted evidence that they had responded to what he had said.

Each term I receive a booklet from Holland Park, a document produced to the highest standards, more what you'd expect from a top hotel than a school. It gives a flavour of how the previous term has gone. It gives the impression of a comprehensive school with elitist aspirations, if you know what I mean. They unashamedly boast of the universities their students have gone to, they talk about the important people who have visited the school, they brag about the talent pool of staff they are developing. They are developing pride in what they are creating. Out of people.

The teachers are the smartest professionals you will come across outside of banking. Dark suits are the order of the day. Sixth-formers dress the same way as staff, and they eat in the same canteen as staff. All of this is quite deliberate, as they want these young people to copy the superb staff they have. Colin boasts as much of the exalted academic backgrounds of his teachers as the poshest independent school might do. And boy, does he work his teachers hard. They are in at 7.30 am and still there well into the evening. On Saturday, extra classes are run, and the school is abuzz. I watched one teacher of English taking a lesson and noticed that she was quite elderly. Oh yes, says Colin, Bridget is well into her seventies, but one of the most effective teachers he has ever come across. She's happy to carry on until she drops, he adds. If the boys from the local council estate fail to turn up to her extra English lessons on Saturday morning, she knocks on their door and escorts them back to her class. Parents are in awe of her. So are the students, who do exceedingly well under her tutelage.

Colin's associate head, or 'Head of Academy', David, could have been a leading architect or interior designer. His mark is everywhere, and the school is a stunning environment. You walk through the building and get the sense of what an enormous privilege it would be to study here.

There is no rubbish on the walls, no 'Ofsted outstanding' banners draped across the gates. We are in a high-class establishment. You feel smart just walking through the corridors.

I like working in The Key's smart offices. They say something about my organisation, of how we like to work, of how we treat our staff. Walk through Holland Park and the abiding impression you are left with is of quality, high standards, attention to detail. I visited Sandfield primary school in Guildford recently and had a similar impression, even though the school is housed in a very lived-in Victorian building. St Stephen's Junior School in Canterbury is the same. It doesn't smell of school; it is smart and has its own personality. Shenley Brook End in Milton Keynes or Wade Deacon High School in Widnes are among my favourite school sites. Entering Wade Deacon is like walking into a university. It looks like a serious education establishment: smart, calm, spacious.

I remember how privileged I felt when the school where I started teaching built a new block and I was invited by the head to move into it. I made sure that my classroom was superb. I was given some wooden staging that fit together like Lego that I used to get children to practise speaking on a public platform. I had loads of wall space which I could use for all sorts of displays. Because I felt special, I made sure that the kids felt the same.

Colin Hall led a school assembly when I was visiting Holland Park with a team of people from The Key. The students walked into the room in silence. As I recall, candles lit up the alcoves that punctuated the walls. The room had low lighting and a huge dramatic PowerPoint image dominated the enormous screen at the front. The dramatic atmosphere was carefully constructed so that everyone knew that something of importance was about to happen.

Teachers have enormous power and Colin recognises this more than most people I know. He has built an environment where that power can be exploited to the full, leading to rich learning experiences for everyone who works there, staff and students alike. In our schools we can create something exceedingly special for staff and pupils. Expect great things in an environment that screams excellence and you shouldn't be surprised when you strike gold.

Bad teaching - no names

Bad teaching damages pupils... sometimes for life. I am not trying to be melodramatic. The science teacher I had from the ages of 11 to 13 completely convinced me that I hated science and really wasn't capable of it anyway. This meant that when I moved schools and received very average science teaching I continued with my negative thoughts about the subject which the teachers failed to repair. Am I right to blame the teacher? Well? Who else is there? Should I blame my 13-year-old self? Well, to some extent, but the teachers failed me.

I have since learned that I tend to be a big-picture thinker and need to see the point of anything I am studying. Connect me with something bigger or deeper and I am engaged. When studying for my undergraduate finals I had to draw an overview of each Shakespeare play on a single sheet of A3. I have taken the same approach ever since. Only the other day I asked our chief marketing officer to draw on a whiteboard how she saw our strategy developing over the next year. Once she had shown me how everything interconnected, I was highly engaged and committed.

But my science teachers never seemed to think they had to do this. If the physics teacher had only spoken about how his subject was all about how the world works, I would have been intrigued. If he'd spoken about energy as the force behind the universe, I'd have concentrated. But all I was told was that $E = mc^2$. What on earth did that mean? Booooring. Was it too much to ask that the teacher should figure out how to ensure every pupil, me in particular, engaged with their subject?

If the teacher is so enthused by their subject anyway, it shows. They don't really need to work so hard. The enthusiasm passes through all their communication and wakens any unresponding pupil – or, at the very least, it helps.

It takes a particularly competent teacher – probably great rather than good (look up Jim Collins's longitudinal study of great companies, called *Good to Great*) – to turn around a pupil who has already gone into negative mode with a previous teacher. There is a bolshiness required, a refusal to accept the attitude they see in front of them, a brilliance perhaps. That is the kind of teaching that requires experience. Sadly, teaching that is 'good enough' has been the focus of too many schools over the last decade or so as they seek to play the game of pleasing the inspectorate. I'll say more about this later.

But allow me to rant a bit about my own profession. I know teaching is exhausting and requires huge mental effort to do well. But if that is the profession you have chosen, you have a duty to do it exceedingly well. We don't want our doctors or dentists to be *good enough*; they need to be excellent. Headteachers should put you in the position where this is possible, demanding only the minimum from you by way of proof of the progress that your students are making. Your job is to engage your charges and take them on a learning journey where they fully understand the different constructs necessary to master your subject at the level required. It's a tough gig, but it's also one of the most privileged jobs you could have. The understanding and competence you inculcate in your pupils is of extremely high value, like gold.

Some headteachers shy away from demanding particularly high standards from their staff. They worry that they'll get into trouble with the unions. That is nonsense. I know most of the union leaders and they are absolutely committed to the highest standards in the profession. They just want teachers to have the tools and resources to do their job effectively and they don't want teachers to be judged poorly if they don't have these. And talking of unions, Ontario, which has one of the highest-performing school systems in the world, puts its success down in large part to the excellent relationship between the ministry, the management and the unions. Headteachers should have no excuses as to why they demand anything less than excellent teaching. They should be hugely proud of doing so. Today's millennial generation want to achieve mastery, according to Daniel Pink in his excellent book, *Drive*. So, headteachers need to help them with that. Professional development should be woven into the working week of the school, not left to the beginning of term or the occasional training day. Teachers want to excel. They are learners before they are teachers, and schools should realise that.

Schools need to refresh teachers. However good you are at it, let's acknowledge that teaching is very tiring. The groups of schools that are coming together around the country should enable teachers who are nearing burn-out to move to a different, less-demanding role to recover for a year or two. The alternative is that we carry on losing between 40% and 50% of teachers within five years of them embarking on their careers. We must be able to figure out how to deal with this situation.

My A level history teacher was just a tad mechanistic in his approach. He was so eccentric that it was actually comical. A tall, black-clad, thick-lens-wearing priest would walk into the lesson. Don't get me wrong here – he was a gentle and caring guy. But he'd walk in and stand at the front without looking at us and it would go like this:

Name of the Father and of the Son and of the Holy Ghost Amen Hail Mary full of grace the Lord is with thee blessed art thou amongst women Holy Mary mother of God pray for us sinners now and at the hour of our death Amen Thomas Cromwell was the main mover in the dissolution of the monasteries. He was under pressure to find the revenues for a depleted treasury...

Occasionally he would look up to see if we were still there. He would dictate to us for the whole lesson and we would write down what he said. He would set us an essay each week, mark it overnight (impressive), and at the bottom of your essay would write...

B+ Good

(less impressive). That was it. No other comment. How were we to learn anything from that? It would take you about four hours to research and write, but the teacher would give you next to no feedback. How could you improve your grade? It was all guesswork. It makes me frustrated that anyone could have thought that this acceptable.

The crazy thing here is that the teacher worked doggedly to prepare his material and mark our work, but his efforts bore little relation to the learning that came from what he was doing. If only he had stopped to reflect on how he could have got more bang for his buck, we would all have benefited. Were we engaged in the lessons? He didn't know, because he barely looked at us. A few of the students simply went away and learnt everything he had given us for the exam, and did well. But not a single one went on to study history. What a waste.

Philippa Walker – getting organised

I nearly cried when one of our best researchers at The Key told me she had decided to leave. What made it worse was that she was leaving to train as an English teacher, so I couldn't even complain. I have always said that it would be greatly hypocritical on my part if I bemoaned any of our people joining or going back to the profession we were trying our hardest to support. But I was still upset.

At least I was able to influence where she actually went, however, in terms of school. She ended up training at SJB, as everyone locally knows St John the Baptist Catholic School in Woking, run by Ani Magill, one of the strongest heads of her generation. Philippa is one of the nicest, brightest, most organised people I have come across. And 'nicest' isn't a term used for many teachers outside the fictional world of Miss Honey.

After a year or so, I asked Ani how Philippa was getting on. 'She's stunning,' she replied.

No chance of getting her back, then.

I caught up with Philippa a year or so after that. Amongst other things, I was fascinated to know how she was managing her time, particularly when the media have been so full of stories of teachers leaving the profession because the workload is too great. I was delighted to hear that the school looks down on people taking work home as a norm. Instead, it is the expectation that a teacher should be able to fit their work into a long day. Philippa told me that she arrives at 7.30 am and tries to get away by 6/6.30. Remember, she is an English teacher: in other words, she has a bigger marking load than just about any other subject. Having to mark extended essays for GCSE, for example, is a huge challenge. But Philippa organises herself so that she can do this during the school day, and the school culture facilitates this.

She has now taught for about three years. She loves it. She really enjoys getting stuck into teaching literature that she enjoys, which is one of the main reasons she went into the job in the first place. It is pretty much what she was expecting, she says. You just have to be so disciplined, if you want to enjoy it. You need a plan for how you are going to spend every minute when you are not actually teaching. Figure out what is going to be of value, and what isn't.

Oliver Burkeman's podcast *Fetishising Busyness* is particularly pertinent to teachers. He argues that it is human nature to be more impressed with the effort that something takes than the particular outcome it produces. Slave through 30 books and spend ten minutes on each one as you prove to yourself how thorough a teacher you are. Are those 300 minutes of your time producing the best learning for your students that they could be, or could you try a different way and do so much better? Mark Enser (@EnserMark) writes a blog he calls *Teach Real* and wrote a particular post titled 'Keep Calm and Just Teach' where he shockingly says:

> Generally I find I am very relaxed about my job and have a pretty good work/life balance. I like to get into work early (about 7 am) but if I don't have a meeting I am often out the door at 3.30 pm and home in time for a run. I might do a little work in the evening but it tends to be marking a few tests, researching a topic I am teaching or looking through some plans. Things I can do while relaxing in front of the TV.

I told you it was shocking, indolent even. He argues that you should collaborate on planning, sharing out as much as possible, that you should use your network to find resources. He rarely puts written comments on work in books, but looks at them and notes the common issues the class as a whole have got. He circulates while pupils are working and gives feedback as the work is being done. He uses quizzes that students can mark for themselves to spot the common problems that need addressing. As a head of geography he has stopped doing expensive trips that only the better-off students can afford and spends a fraction of the energy required on these to organise local projects instead. He doesn't put up elaborate displays in his classroom ('they quickly become background, a visual white noise'). He offers other advice, which is well worth noting.

Mr Pinkett (@positivteacha), the head of English at King's College in Guildford, argues that English teachers do far too much marking and that much of it is not particularly useful in terms of feedback to the student. He advocates, and practises, *only* focusing on specific elements of a student's work that you are working on at that time. In this way, the teacher doesn't get distracted from the specific learning intentions of the piece of work (for example by looking at the spelling or the punctuation), and the teacher benefits from the acute focus on the learning topic. I get that, but it is very hard to achieve. Bearing in mind, however, that the English teacher's work can be quite crippling, it is well worth the effort to ensure marking has maximum value.

I remember in my first (and, to be honest, my second) year of teaching being quite ridiculously anal about marking. It was a point of pride to me that a) there would be lots of work in the pupils' books; and b) it would all be marked; and c) I would mark thoroughly and personally to the child. I used to write acronyms in the margin that the child could only work out by coming to speak to me. OTIAECOLMLO would clearly mean 'Oh that is an excellent choice of language, my little one'. It generated a bit of fun, but ended up consuming even more time. I wouldn't hand in the half-term data until I had marked the final set of books. So, marking the books would take about two hours. Then I'd write the reports. I'd be up working 'til 2 or 3 in the morning. Not very clever. But I reckon I enjoyed the martyr feeling. Really, not very clever.

Teachers who want to keep on enjoying their jobs have got to adopt a *modus operandi* that brings about effective learning, not that impresses senior managers or school inspectors or fuels their martyr complex. The teacher is a professional, and professionals make their own (evidence-based, for sure) choices as to how to do their jobs.

I wish I had been more like Philippa when I was teaching. Maybe…
But that's not worth thinking about.

The classroom – your country, your kingdom

When I was a headteacher, I carried on teaching, but never subsequently had my own classroom. It was never the same. I was squatting in someone else's and I couldn't put my whole personality into the space. I loved having my own classroom as a teacher. I couldn't believe that I had been given control over my own space. I stood in it before the beginning of my first term, imagining the possibilities. And my first classroom was so small it barely fitted about four rows of desks. But it was mine, and I could use it to make dreams come alive. I really did think like that.

It was my kingdom and I was going to set the rules. OK, so I obviously had to follow the general rules and policies set by the school (although I never remember reading any kind of staff handbook when I started). But I could do so much within that framework. I would decide how the pupils were going to enter the classroom, where they would sit and what the behaviour norms were going to be.

I liked to make all of this fiendishly complicated. Now, I've got you… why would I make it complicated? Well, I wanted kids to have to work out how to succeed in the systems I set. In one particular year, I was fed up of the year 7s running to my room and being over-excited, so as I explained earlier, every lesson began with two minutes of silence, when they all had to put their heads on their desks. I had a two-minute silence monitor, who would be rewarded with classroom points (I'll explain later) for doing a good job, or sacked for not being precise enough. I wanted to sharpen concentration amongst one class, so I had certain trigger words that required a particular response, a bit like when radio stations want you to ring in when you hear certain songs. Another year I decided that the boys I was teaching were behind other year groups in terms of their ability to write coherent sentences. So, the obvious solution was to start every lesson with two minutes of jabbering, yes? I know I've mentioned this earlier in the book, but you've probably forgotten what I was talking about. Jabbering was where each person put pen to paper and wrote continuously for an allotted period of time (two or three minutes). If they couldn't think of anything to write, then they had to put, 'I can't think of anything to write...'

I noticed that one year group was ridiculously competitive. So, I set up a classroom points system where they got points for lots of different things, but so did I. At the end of the half-term, whoever was in the lead would receive a reward, probably edible. *My* reward, if I won, might be to entertain the class to an extra half-hour of work one breaktime.

I liked encouraging pupils, so I'd reward a good answer with a two-second applause, which the class would provide, starting and finishing exactly when I said so. OK, so you think I'm a power-crazed control freak. You may well be right, but I loved it and, from the feedback I got (in a roundabout way), so did the kids. It kept them on their toes. They had to be constantly prepared. I was able to keep them pretty sharp.

I love visiting schools and seeing the equivalent of my rather idiosyncratic systems still thriving today. They teach children to work out the different expectations of different social contexts. Miss O'Malley expects you to have your homework open on your desks at the start of the lesson, while Mr Dhatt wants you to stand behind your desk before he invites you to sit down and unpack your things. The teacher sets the norms; the pupil has to understand and keep to them.

I wanted my classroom to fit with my character. If I leaned towards the uber-controlling, then so be it. Others were far more laid-back, and that worked, too. I wanted lots of flexibility in my room, so I bribed the children with classroom points if they could reorganise, in complete silence, all the tables into the new shape I had drawn on the whiteboard within the time I gave them. If they could predict beforehand exactly, to the second, how long it was going to take them, I added points. If they could do it too easily, I added complexity: Ali had to end up sitting two desks away from David; Carys had to be four desks to the left of Josh. It meant they had to work well as a group; they could collaborate using non-verbal communication only. And it was entertaining for me to watch them.

Styles can differ. One literature class I watched of the senior year (year 13 or upper 6th) in a high school in Walla Walla, Washington state, felt more like a stand-up party at the beginning of the lesson. Students were gathering together, grabbing coffees or 'sodas' from the side of the room and catching up on the previous evening's news while unpacking their books. The teacher wandered up to a lectern, coffee mug in hand, and began the lesson. The kids loved her and, with mock complaint, settled into the seats. There followed the most brilliant summary of the learning so far, together with an explanation of how the piece of work just completed fitted into the overall scheme of work. I got the sense that the teacher kept running through the key points of what the class were learning each lesson, inviting students to tell the story with her.

I was always keen to read as much as I could about new teaching approaches. I remember thinking that I was maybe doing too much from the front of the class, so for the next book that we were going to study (I think it was *The Silver Sword* by Ian Serraillier) I spent much of the holidays preparing exercises that I wanted the pupils to work on in groups. I overdid this, in my keenness to do it well, and the kids became fed up of spending each lesson slaving through the exercises. I later learned to mix things up a bit more, so that the learning experience was more *blended*, to use modern lingo.

You've got to enjoy your teaching. I am working on the assumption that the teacher already loves their subject. That was certainly the case with me. I loved the combination of novels, poems, linguistic complexity that made up the study of English. Then you've got to develop your own style, through a series of experiments. You need to take time to go and watch other teachers from time to time, so that you can challenge your own approach and try adapting it. Finally, you've got to stay up to date with the latest pedagogical ideas. Teaching is complex. If your class is very broad in terms of different individuals' achievement up to that point, then life for the teacher is especially challenging. Others will have made significant progress in trying to crack this particular conundrum, so it's important to find out what they have been doing and see if you can borrow ideas from them. OK, *steal*, but it's a friendly kind of theft.

As much as it's a great joy for a teacher to have their own kingdom, it's also potentially a problem as it can encourage the teacher to become more and more isolated from others. They can easily fall prey to the thinking that theirs is the only way of doing things. Teachers are professionals and, like doctors or accountants or lawyers, they have a duty to stay up to date with the latest educational research and practice. They can only do that by being well read, mixing with other teachers to engage in professional dialogue, visiting other schools and listening to specialists in particular areas of practice so they can keep developing their own style and approach. The world, people and our understanding of them keep changing. Teaching cannot remain effective unless it keeps adapting to that changing world.

Mr Wood – any questions?

I couldn't cope any more with the bouncy, jokey, let's-just-have-a-good-time maths teacher I had when I was 15, so I got my parents to write in to the school and ask that I be moved down from set 2 to set 3 (out of 5), where I knew the highly regarded, if very conservative Mr Wood was the teacher. When it happened, I was delighted and relieved. It was half-way through the year, so I realised that the authorities had bent the rules for me.

For a reason I still don't understand, Mr Wood was known as Drac. Not to his face, you understand: that would have been life-limiting. Certain nicknames seemed to be handed down by the students from one generation to the next. In the class he was Mr Wood, or more often just 'sir'. Outside, it was totally *de rigueur* to refer to him as Drac. Fr Dooley was Norbert; Mr Keating was always Brian; Fr Richmond was Buzz; Fr O'Halloran – Dolly; Mr John – Slug. No one ever dreamt of changing a nickname. That would have broken some kind of ancient protocol that seemed to be part of the school mystique. I guess the staff *must* have known what we called them. Who got to decide originally what the student body was officially going to use as a nickname? No idea, but there was an authority somewhere, and it was a crime to ignore it/him/her/whoever.

Drac was absolutely meticulous in his entire approach. There were rules and you did not break them. If you were late to hand in your homework, you were always sent on a run at breaktime. Fail to set out your work in the 'correct' manner, you did the whole lot again, however successful it might have been. Call out in class and you were forced to stand up for five minutes. But there were benefits. If you didn't understand something when he was explaining it in class, you put your hand up and told him so. If any other student made any kind of comment, or noise, or looked in any way deprecating towards the individual, that was the most sinful thing you could have done. And we all knew it. Consequently, we were well used to going over topics several times, and not continuing until everyone was on the same page.

I loved it. Everything was clear to me. Maybe I actually loved rules; I think I probably did. I loved knowing that if I didn't understand I could pull the stop chain and the class would come to a halt, and no one could give me any grief. It was liberating, and such a contrast to my previous maths set where I sat at the back getting more and more anxious because I didn't understand what was going on.

There wasn't much flexibility in Drac's approach, it is true to say. It was very much chalk and talk. In other words, he explained a topic from the front; we listened and tried to understand; then we did some exercises. Once, I had bought a notebook for all my subjects and was making notes about the rules of quadratic equations or whatever. Mr Wood told me to come up to the front to show him what I was doing. He flicked through the book and saw some material from other subjects and immediately decided that I hadn't been concentrating. Penalty: do a run. But I hadn't been doing other work, I explained. I took the book and opened it to where I had been writing maths. That very act was one of defiance. Arguing with the teacher was a cardinal sin and I was ordered to get three ferulas.

I'd better explain. Until the mid-'80s it was pretty much the norm for any boys' school to have corporal punishment. Corporal, meaning physical (from the Latin *corpus*, obvs, meaning body). In Jesuit schools, there seemed to be a rule that meant that the teacher who wanted you to receive ferulas (or 'cracks' as they were nicknamed) could not also administer the punishment. So, you had to line up after lessons and go to a special room in the school to have the ferulas administered. I hope I am making this sound sufficiently dystopian.

Ferula? This was a sort of bat with rounded ends, about 18 inches long, five inches in width and about half an inch deep. It was black and looked like hardened plastic. On the day before I left school I actually 'borrowed' the ferula out of the deputy head's study. I took it home, gave it to the guy who was going to be my older brother's best man at his forthcoming wedding, who presented it to my brother's new wife during the best man speech with advice on how to keep my brother in order. My brother still has it, if you want it back, guys.

But I digress. I was incensed that I had been ordered ferulas when I had done nothing wrong. But Drac would not entertain any discussion. It's great to have rules, but you also need fairness, and most young people have a very highly developed sense of justice and what does and doesn't meet its standards. For a 15-year-old, that was a hugely stressful event which meant that I didn't sleep. I had to go and knock on the door of the deputy head, to whom I had never spoken. I had to articulate an argument in fumbling speech that got across exactly what the issue was and why I felt it so unfair. I remember him saying that he would discuss the matter with Mr Wood. At the time, that meant that I was not yet off the hook, so I didn't sleep for the next couple of days. And he never came back to me, so I was never sure whether or not my argument had been accepted. Going to the next maths lesson was very anxiety-inducing. And the next one, and the next one, until I finally realised that we had moved on. This was a kind of mental torture and it was wrong of the teachers to put me through it. It might not have been a particularly big deal for them, but to me it was huge.

Anyway, listen, it's all forgotten and forgiven now. Clearly. Mr Wood was a highly effective teacher and I don't think anyone in the class got less than a B in the O level that we all took. And that was when boys were men and Bs meant something, OK?

Developing mystique and reputation

Once you've taught for a few years in the same school, you will have a reputation. Not necessarily a positive one, but you will definitely have one. The students in every school have a highly effective set of jungle drums which pass around their thoughts about teachers more effectively than any other known form of communication. The poor teacher at my secondary school who had once had a psychotic episode and called himself a tree was forever knows as Tree by the cruel kids. But isn't that horrible? Well, kids make judgements which hurt and they are not inclined to forgiveness. It's a pity they are like that and it would be great to modify that attitude, but that is still the norm in most schools I come across. There is an innate conservativeness in the way that pupils think and act. I remembered the fuss I caused when I suggested, at the second school I led, that prefects might be selected in a different way from how it had been done for decades. There was uproar. I learnt my lesson and backed down. I didn't have enough political capital at that stage to make such a symbolic move. It takes time and stealth to change the fundamental way in which people think and act, particularly in the tribal setting of a school.

When I was at secondary school myself, it seemed that very few teachers came to the school just for a short time. Most had been there for years already or were destined to stay there for years to come. A few went on to be heads at other schools, but I really don't remember there being much turnover other than that. What a pity, in some ways. My eldest daughter went to a leading independent school for part of her schooling. Its exam results always secured top-ten placings in the league tables. But its physics teachers, almost invariably of poor quality, seemed to last for a year at best. It was a running joke among the students that the beginning-of-year ritual would involve being introduced to their new physics teacher. Good science teachers today are fêted by schools as celebrities, they are becoming so rare. Even those schools with the starriest academic reputations find it nigh-on impossible to attract strong scientists to work for them. Teaching science just hasn't managed to make itself sexy, as it should have done.

If we simply think of what has been invented over the past few years that we now take for granted – the ubiquitous GPS apps that we all rely on, iPhones that give us instant access to any information we want via 'Siri', vacuum cleaners that have more sucking power than anything you can think of, or the eradication of polio or the huge reduction in malaria in Africa brought about by the work of the Gates Foundation, or self-driving cars – surely science automatically becomes hugely fascinating? How did all of this happen? What discoveries made them possible? Surely science is the most magical subject area in the school curriculum! Science teachers should think of themselves as scientists first and teachers second. They should constantly be collecting *Why?* questions from the world around them. They should explain the maths behind space exploration, or why combine harvesters have doubled farm yields over the past 20 years, or why deadly tsunamis happen. The world is an endlessly fascinating and dangerous and amazing place. I fail to understand why we have not managed to attract more scientists into schools to share their fascination and try to explain some of the phenomena. They don't all have to possess the charisma of a Robert Winston or Susan Greenfield (although it would help), but they do need to be fascinated. I suspect the problem is in large part down to the fact that so few headteachers are trained scientists. Your typical school leader has an arts degree – probably English. Is it any wonder, then, that science is not prioritised?

I consider my own science education: both my parents doctors, yet I was totally switched off. Why do schools find it acceptable to put mediocre teachers into its science departments? At the secondary school in Brixton whose governing body I chaired for six years, I questioned the head as to why we were keeping one of the teachers whose lessons were consistently inadequate or barely adequate. He told me that they had tried to recruit someone better, but failed. Many schools have brought in science teachers from the Far East, but anecdotal feedback would suggest that this is no panacea as linguistic and cultural issues often make the transition less successful than was hoped for. The principal argued that a bad teacher was better than no teacher. I told him how much I disagreed, and pointed to research aggregations from the Education Endowment Foundation that backed up my position. I argued that, as a temporary measure, we'd be better off having one really good science teacher teaching classes of 50 or 60 than submit 25/30 students to what we knew was poor teaching. In the end we employed a science graduate, with no teaching qualification, to support the work of the very successful science teacher in the next class, and they worked closely together. I believe the unqualified teacher then trained and achieved qualified teacher status shortly afterwards.

But back to reputation. For those who hadn't quite won over the affections of their charges in their early years, teaching could mean a long sentence. Some of the teacher nicknames included 'Slug', 'Killer', 'Dolly', 'Bossy', 'Laz'. If you *did* manage to win affection, then you were known by your first name. If not, then you were condemned without mercy.

A reputation can be very helpful, of course. If you are known to be a strict disciplinarian, the pupils are already appropriately wary of you before you even started teaching them. You have relatively little problem with classroom control, but you will have to draw the more anxious children out of themselves if you want to engage them, of course.

It's why I determined to be very strict in my first few years of teaching. At times I was probably a bit over-the-top, but I wanted to make it very clear that I wasn't going to take any nonsense. I wanted children to learn at speed, and I couldn't achieve the pace I wanted unless concentration levels were high. Strangely enough, I was never conscious of my nickname at the various schools where I taught, or which I led.

I just hope it was Fergal.

Mr Humphrey – the hard worker

My daughter, Camilla, did very well at school, academically. Ask her who inspired her most and she will put her principal A level French teacher, Colin Humphrey, at the top of her list. He was the kind of teacher I love, as I hope by now you are well aware: far from perfect, but absolutely brilliant.

Actually, I love the fact that it was so easy to see Colin's flaws: fussy, anxious, impatient, prone to stress – I recognised all of this as soon as I met him. But he was also one of the best teachers I have ever come across. Great teachers are rarely perfect humans. Good job.

He was devoted to his subject and his students, and was hugely ambitious for them. High expectations were core to his approach. He worked exceptionally hard. He treated each student as an individual with their own set of needs. So, he recognised that Camilla was well ahead in her study of the subject. She had been to a bilingual nursery where as a three-year-old she had learned all her nursery rhymes in French and was used to hearing French spoken for most of every morning. Colin pushed her hard and made it clear that he expected her to work to A* standard from the off. Her reaction, predictably, was a mixture of excitement and resentment.

I wonder whether he worked *too* hard. I can only imagine that he did several hours each evening in order to mark work in the way he did, and to prepare the kinds of lessons he planned. I am not praising this, as I am convinced that you can be a highly effective teacher without working

12-hour days. Teaching lessons is an exhausting exercise that demands mentally-draining energy in a way that few other work activities do, and teachers need to build in daily restoration that does not depend on too much Malbec, as well as giving themselves time for planning and assessing. They have to be organised, and their organisation must include proper rest and recovery time. Too many teachers fail to recognise the exhausting nature of their jobs. They end up eating biscuits to keep their sugar levels up, which increases their weight, which increases their tiredness... and so on and so on. New teachers in particular need to think carefully how they are going to organise each day, so that they can manage and stay energised.

OK, I know this is now getting rather nerdy, but my own working day took a turn for the better when I changed what I ate for breakfast. I now have a huge bowl of bran flakes with muesli on top. I use almond or soya milk (I did warn you this was getting strange) and I put a good three heaped dessert spoonsful of Yeo Valley organic natural yogurt on top. This mixture is great. The bran flakes have lots of magnesium in them, which helps with your mental health in as much as I think it's meant to reduce any propensity to depression you might have. The muesli makes it taste nice, and the yogurt and milk give you slow-release energy over a good number of hours. Ever since I have had this breakfast, which I stick to religiously I have to admit (much to the amusement and scorn of my family), I have kept my weight down and my energy up. There – you have now managed to wangle an intimate secret out of me. But I'm not promising any others.

Anyway, back to Colin. He was the model of thoroughness. He knew what he wanted to achieve in his lessons. He always gave a sense that time was short and that each minute needed to be used effectively. I remember him telling Camilla exactly how many weeks she had before mocks, or AS exams or A2s. He knew exactly what they would be doing as a class each week and gave the students a sense of urgency that was constantly present in the conversations I overheard them having.

Colin built a programme of lessons using videos of the news in French that was designed to increase the students' fluency in the language. They watched the events of the day in the language they were trying to learn, noting down the words and phrases in current usage, discussing the different way the French chose to express themselves in contrast to the English. The dominant issues were woven into the themes dictated by the exam syllabus they were following. He explained how to impress the examiner by using certain constructions and idioms. He gave them checklists, so they had a structured plan of what they had to learn each week. They were given a sense of progressing towards the target. He told them every few weeks what grade they were now working to. I remember Camilla showing me his comments at the bottom of a piece of work she had written. At the bottom of a whole paragraph of feedback, he had written: 'A*, but not Oxbridge quality'. Don't you just love it? As Camilla subsequently discovered, he actually took them well ahead of the grade he led them to think they were on, and several of them got A*s and As in the actual final exams.

Unsurprisingly, several of the students went on to study French at university, where they found themselves well prepared for the course ahead of them.

Colin was the one teacher for whom Camilla insisted we needed to buy a present. When she went in to give it to him, she said he became quite tearful he was so grateful. I don't think he really understood quite what he had done for her. So it's worth rehearsing exactly that.

Under Colin's tutelage, Camilla was given a sense of structure, of urgency, of momentum. She learnt to be thorough and organised. Because they were learning so much so quickly, she developed a sense of competence that made her feel good about herself. So, her self-esteem grew. She and her peers learned to treat learning itself as being of huge importance. When the rest of the school stayed at home for a snow day, he persuaded the whole class to show up for a lesson because, he argued, it was critical and they couldn't afford to miss it. He and Bridget, from Holland Park, were peas in a pod on this score.

But students never really know how to articulate what their teacher has done for them. It's taken me decades to realise what mine did for me, for goodness' sake. But it's well worth the exercise. Teachers like Colin have a huge impact on young people, and I am eternally grateful to him for what he did for my daughter. I just hope he retired with a strong sense of the impact he had made on so many young people's lives.

Why teaching is more complex than knee surgery

One of the problems I have with the Teach First programme, where UK graduates with strong academic results are placed in schools with significant proportions of disadvantaged children, is that it encourages the teaching profession to be seen as something you join for two, three or four years and then leave to pursue a more 'normal' job once you have earned your spurs. All the teachers in this book spent decades teaching, during which time they became more and more confident as to what worked for them as practitioners. The overall message is that teaching is not something you can pick up quickly and master in a short space of time. It is just too complex.

Firstly, you are faced with so many variables. Every class you have consists of up to 30 different individuals, all coming from different places, with differing needs. You have different curricula and exam syllabi to learn *yourself* before you can teach them. With the much higher survival rates of premature babies, you are increasingly likely to have children with special educational needs in your class because special schools take only the most severely needy children these days. You may have a teaching assistant whom you need to manage if they are to impact effectively on your class's learning. The head of your school is likely to change more regularly than used to be the case, now every five years rather than seven a few years ago. And you need to have developed a bedrock of confidence if a visit from the school inspectors is not to cause you undue stress. The mention of knee surgery in the title of this chapter comes from a conference I was at some years ago where I attended a breakfast session at 8 am, not something I am routinely inclined to do, especially after the conference dinner the night before, which was never teetotal. Professor Brent Davies was trying to shock us into giving us his full attention and in doing so, compared the challenge of the knee surgeon with that of the teacher. His point was to emphasise quite how complex the role of the teacher is, and how we need to treat such a role with more respect. It is so complex as to require much more weight and experience, in the same way that the surgeon needs to have studied a great deal and proved themselves over many years before they are given the chance to work unsupervised.

The trouble in England and Wales at the moment is that only about half the profession has more than ten years' experience. So many school staff rooms, particularly in urban areas which are more prone to higher mobility, are full of teachers in their twenties. This is particularly the case in London and the south-east, where it is so expensive to buy or rent a house and raise a family. We have real issues when it comes to developing experience in the profession, and we need to deal with this.

Earlier in the book we were talking about the challenge of turning around demotivated students. Teachers with significant years of experience are more likely to have figured out how and why children have developed negative attitudes about themselves. They can more readily spot the tell-tale signs: the class joker who has adopted an alternative role to that of learner (where she feels incompetent); the pupil who never looks the teacher in the eye; the constant talker or fiddler; the child who tries everything to miss school, or your lesson, for a variety of reasons. So often these camouflage the real issues going on underneath, and the more experienced teacher is usually quicker to realise what is going on.

The more experienced teacher should, in any case, be a lot more adept at ensuring that no student is switched off in the first place. This is a tough challenge. Some will be so engaged in your lesson that they want to dominate discussion, put their hand up for everything, constantly ask you questions. It is easy for the teacher to be so taken up with these children that they pay much less attention to the others. The more weathered teacher has eyes everywhere, *à la* Terry Brooks, spotting the signs, teasing the timid into speaking, using different devices to engage quieter kids, turning disruptive individuals into leaders. It is highly skilled work and too difficult and important to reserve for novices.

The classroom environment is a dynamic one. Children can develop at pace. If you have a seven-year-old for a year in your class, that's a huge fraction of their entire lifetime to date. The younger the child, the greater the rate at which their brains are changing. Of course, we know now that brains are hugely plastic, and the teacher can do so much to make them even more so. Term three, for the seven-year-old, should feel light years away from term one, because the demands from the teacher and the programme of study are so much greater. Skills acquired in harmony for the music student in term one should be turned into superb performances in term three. The teacher layers learning so that each subsequent layer is dependent on the underlying one. Not all the children will acquire these layers at the same time, so the teacher has to deal with taking them from multiple points on the journey. He has to remain calm, when classes can become difficult and at times appear chaotic. If he waits for all the children to get to the same place, you can pretty much guarantee that he will have switched off those children who got there first. If you don't keep the pace up as a teacher, you lose the attention of the quickest thinkers in the class. Slower thinkers should not be dismissed as less intelligent, as the latest personality tests demonstrate. But they require a different approach. The strongest teachers can put together lessons that engage every type of learning and every different standpoint in terms of attitude.

You can maybe begin to accept quite how complicated the teacher's role turns out to be. Great teaching is not at all easily achieved. In fact, I reckon that *competent* teaching is the norm is most schools, but great teaching is relatively scarce, quite simply because it is so very difficult to achieve. Too often school leaders are happy to have teachers who are *good enough*. That is a shame. Every school needs as many great teachers as it can produce. Heads should look at their staff and ask themselves who looks as if they might have the potential to be great. Then they need to invest behind them. Maybe all teachers should be on that journey; I'm not sure. Great teaching is so finely tuned and so difficult to achieve that teachers who achieve it should certainly be recognised for it. Higher pay, for sure. Greater responsibility? Possibly, as it will be such teachers who are the most effective role models for other teachers who are on the journey.

But we cannot put up with bare competence. That is to dismiss the profession as one where mediocrity is perfectly acceptable. We need to reorient our perspectives so that we see teaching as a journey towards exceptional performance as the norm. Those who achieve this should be the leaders in the profession. Leaders, not middle leaders. Headteachers are not necessarily focused on great teaching. They may not have been great teachers themselves.

Teachers challenge the thinking of others: that's their fundamental job. Sometimes this role extends beyond the classroom. The whole issue of special needs is a sensitive one and I realise that one has to tread carefully. But there came a point in my dealings with one parent of a child with Asperger's syndrome where I became very frustrated with the way his mother was treating him. I was the head of the school and every conversation I had with her was dominated by her talking about her son entirely in terms of his 'being Aspergers'. I remember the shock on her face when at one point I told her that her son had the driest sense of humour of any child I had taught, had the quickest comebacks on comments made in class, had the stubbornness of a mule and, well, he was a personality before he was a special need. She looked at me quizzically. I told her that we were in the business of educating the *whole* person and not just a particular facet of that personality. Bearing in mind that she was an intimidating person, it was bold on my part, but it's our job as educators to speak the truth to people, however difficult it might be for the recipient to hear. As it happened, of course, once she had got over my forthrightness, I was her favourite person and her son did outstandingly well in his remaining time at the school.

Is it mad to suggest that schools be run by great teachers? Couldn't four or five of them come together in the way that GPs do, with the support infrastructure run by administrators? At the moment, the role of headteacher or principal does not have pedagogy as its leading component. Is it any wonder, therefore, that great teaching rarely gets a mention?

But it needs to.

Dr Barras – you will not fail

My son's A level English teacher was quite extraordinary. Parents waiting to see her at parent/teacher consultations looked visibly anxious. What was she going to say to you? Would she comment on how you weren't doing enough to help your child succeed? What work would she be insisting happened across the holidays?

As an experienced teacher and headteacher, I found myself just as anxious. Ridiculous. Why did I feel this way? Well, the consultation was in fact a lecture on what your child, and you, could do to make sure that you didn't let their stats down. None of her students had got less than an A in the last three years. Were you and your child going to sully that achievement? Talk about pressure.

She made us look at the anthology of poems that was being studied, then at some of the work that Marcus had submitted lately. She pointed out what she had explained to him/them in class and how Marcus had failed to deliver exactly what she wanted. She looked at us, as if to ask why we were allowing this to happen. She assumed we were deeply involved in his learning and connected with the detail of what he was doing. What did we have to say? Come on.

I once asked a friend how her parenting strategy might be described and she replied without a blink: 'Benign neglect'. I suspect that this is common amongst the majority of parents. But Dr Barras clearly thought it was completely unacceptable. This was a serious exercise. A levels were the gateway to university. Did we not realise that if Marcus didn't do what she told him to do, he wouldn't get the result he was capable of achieving? Quite clearly she was amazed at our negligence. She suggested we might consider reading the main critics on Conrad, one of the authors they were studying. Who might that be, I asked? Well, Dr Barras replied, she herself was one of them and we should think about reading her work. Now, hang on a minute. We weren't the student there, Marcus was. Clearly we were missing the point.

Marcus had ten copies of each poem they had on the list and on each he wrote a set of comments related to a particular theme or poetic element. So, all in all, he had well over a hundred pieces of paper he was using to revise just one section of his A level English syllabus. That's what I call thorough. The study of literature, according to Dr Barras, was as much a technical as an artistic endeavour. It required a disciplined acquiring of analytical skills, and needed time and hard work. She refused to accept that this was beyond what a 17-year-old might be willing to give. She simply assumed that they, and their parents, would sign up to her approach. She took no prisoners and saw no need to do so; it was her way or the highway, to quote the modern day proverb. She knew she was a brilliant teacher. She knew the students were capable of achieving the highest results. She allowed for no other outcomes than top grades.

But this was not down to luck or good fortune, as many students believe. You can pretty much guarantee you'll get the top result if you've done the work. So, do the work. Simples. She showed them how to *do the work* in the most thorough way possible, and she made sure they did. Consequently, she showed not the slightest surprise when all her students succeeded.

I ended up loving this approach and wondering why I hadn't taken exactly the same attitude when I was a teacher. Why did I teach the pupils, then leave it to them to prepare themselves for exams? That's not what Peter Hardwick did when he taught me English A level. He made sure we understood every single nuance of every major soliloquy in the Shakespeare plays we were studying. We had to work blooming hard to do so, for sure. But he set the framework. As did Dr Barras. That's what we mean by *mastery* in today's terms. It's where the teacher ensures that every student has totally understood and can demonstrate their understanding of every construct, or learning point, of the subject being studied. It is not down to chance in any way. There is almost no need for the exam, as the teacher already knows exactly what the students can do.

This takes an intense programme of work, usually involving a 'snowball rolling down the hill' approach, where you make progress, but keep going over previous ground to ensure that knowledge already acquired is bedded in. This was Terry Brooks's approach with Roman history, giving us quick tests every so often to make sure we hadn't forgotten anything. It was Jeremy Attlee's approach in Spanish. It doesn't have to be tedious, although there is inevitably something more humdrum and less entertaining about this aspect of learning. But, as Dr Barras would argue, that's life. If you want something badly enough, you have to work hard for it. Don't expect it to come easily to you, simply because you have an ability or whatever. Teachers who take this approach make big demands on their students. One thing I commented upon after I had watched six outstanding lessons in the school I visited as a new governor was how hard the young people had had to work during each one. Great teachers make their students work. The teacher is not there to entertain, and the students are not there to be entertained. Let's get this straight.

In Dr Barras's world, nothing is left to chance. Rigour and hard work is what works. I hope that Marcus has learnt this for good.

School culture

The witches mumble horrid chants,
You're scolded by five thousand aunts,
A Martian pulls a fearsome face
And hurls you into Outer Space,
You're tied in front of whistling trains,
A tomahawk has sliced your brains,
The tigers snarl, the giants roar,
You're sat on by a dinosaur.
In vain you're shouting 'Help' and 'Stop',
The walls are spinning like a top,
The earth is melting in the sun
And all the horror's just begun.
And, oh, the screams, the thumping hearts
That awful night before school starts.

Max Fatchen

The world of school and the normal world should be one. They should meld into each other so that you can hardly tell the difference between the one and the other. But they don't. Very sadly. Consequently, when you've been away for a few weeks, both teacher and pupil find it tough to imagine going back into that strange and foreign world, with its weird culture and systems.

I suppose we have roles to play that demand some degree of green room preparation before we go on stage. Jo must become Miss Peters, Josh must become Josh Carlsen in 2P who sits behind Tamsin. The trouble is that whenever I think about roles, I think of straitjackets preventing me from being the person I want to be and doing whatever I want. Oh just to be myself! I am no psychologist, but I'm sure it's healthier for the person we are able to be at work and the person we are at home to be as congruent as possible.

Mask-wearing cannot be good for you. Some schools try to overcome this by abandoning the use of formal titles for staff and just using first names instead. However, a survey I carried out (well, actually, a quick conversation with my youngest daughter Nina) suggested that she preferred it at her secondary school when she was more formal, compared to calling her teachers by their first names at primary school. So I guess that some middle ground is best. Some degree of formality can be quite freeing for a teacher in that they can play the role they want to play without having to reveal their whole lives in front of a class. But, to balance that, teachers who feel free to be themselves in front of a class, within a given code as to how the school expects behaviour between teachers and pupils to be tempered, may find they strike better relationships with their pupils, and that it is easier, therefore, to motivate them.

When I visit schools, I find it very interesting to note the relationship between staff and pupils. The Royal Grammar School in Guildford has always impressed me with the way teachers almost unanimously speak to the boys (it is single sex) in a positive and encouraging way. They assume they are behaving well and trying to do well. In other schools, that is far from being the case, and the impression given can so easily be that pupils are not good enough and aren't behaving well enough. It is striking how the demeanour of a group of teachers can vary so much from one school to another. It changes the atmosphere. The head at the RGS, Jon Cox, is quiet, has a very dry sense of humour, but always speaks of his students in the most positive way, without appearing to manufacture his remarks. The environment is, to some extent, set by the tenor of the conversations that are most commonplace within it. But buildings make a difference too, of course.

It doesn't help that so many UK schools have begun to look like penitentiaries. In our effort to keep children safe, we have built high fences and security systems worthy of the Royal Mint, which reinforce the separation of worlds between the outside and inside. Surely we can design safety solutions that don't require students to be caged? We want to teach children in such a way that they don't feel the need to behave differently outside the school as inside. Break down the divide between the two worlds. Ask any school in a tough area how they have improved children's attitudes to learning and it will invariably include actions they have taken to bridge the worlds of home and school. Certain staff will have visited families at home to discuss what will happen when the child starts. Events will have been held which are designed specifically to bring parents into an environment that they had feared when they were children themselves. At the Brixton school, where I was chair of governors for six years, we spent a fair bit of cash on pizza, as we knew that parents thought it was great that we were offering something they loved. We measured ourselves on parental engagement and worked enormously hard to do better at it.

Schools should audit themselves to spot the many weird things they do to create barriers without realising it. Get people who have nothing to do with the school, but who represent the sort of parents the school wants to attract, to look at your website, the uniform, to hang around the local area 20 minutes after finishing time, to approach the school, ring the bell (or whatever), ask to see someone. Without being shown around by anyone official, enable them to have a good look around. Record their impressions. Ask them to rate how happy about the school they feel on a 1-10 scale at each point. Get them to say why. I guarantee that you will find this very eye-opening, if not rather embarrassing.

It is amazing how apparently little things can have quite a significant impact on people's impression of an organisation. Hold events for the community. Get your children out into the community. Connect them to local businesses. Get them to see how 'normal' people behave. If you have children who have become disengaged, get non-teachers (it's important that they don't treat the children as pupils but as ordinary people) to take them to see inspiring people doing impressive things in the local area, particularly those who come from a similar background. Then get the students to act as ambassadors of that local community back in the school, talking to their peers about what they have learned. Have a look at the Bryanston Square 'Unlock' programme (www.bryanstonsquare. com) which has had impressive results in this regard.

It's well worth spending a lot of time stripping away the barriers to learning that schools create without realising it. Start with the smell. Christmas Day in the Roche household when I was growing up would include being taken to the maternity unit where my dad was an obstetrician and, on one occasion, my mum took us around one of the anaesthetic rooms where she worked. The smell of hospitals had such a negative impact on me that I was forever fearful of being in one, and the idea of ever becoming a doctor was anathema to me. Schools can smell badly, too. To be fair, none of the schools I have visited in the last year or so have given out negative olfactory vibes, which is encouraging. But so many people talk about the antiseptic or vegetable-steam smells that pervaded their memories of school that it is clearly a dominant factor in their experience. Changing rooms come high on the list of offensive areas of the school site. It doesn't take industrial quantities of Febreze to deal with the problem. But don't ignore the issue. Sort it out. It can really be offensive. Anyway, I'm not going to take you on a tour of the school. I'm sure you've got the picture. Or the smell. Whatever.

Staffrooms can be so weird. Sort out what they are for, and design them around that purpose. Are they for relaxing and getting away from work, or are they for staff to have quiet areas to plan and prepare? Don't mix those two things together or you'll end up with an unsatisfying mishmash of both. Territory should not be claimed by individuals – the 'that's Jack's chair' scenario, for example – or you risk developing an exclusive and intimidating atmosphere that is off-putting for new colleagues. So easily, little quirks can creep into an organisation. They fester. Somehow, it's worth trying to spring clean a culture. Use Survey Monkey to find out what people really think, assuring confidentiality as you do so. Teachers can do this with their pupils. (Those schools that really listen to their children achieve more than others, because they are serving their constituents more effectively. It's not rocket science.) Teachers should regularly be able to give voice to the way they are feeling, and school leaders would do very well to listen hard. If you want your school to be oriented around teachers and teaching, then listening to teachers must be a given.

Schools develop their own events and rituals that are important to generations of pupils. Christmas lunch seemed to be universally loved in the schools where I have worked. The staff pantomime can be a chance for teachers to show that they don't *really* take themselves too seriously. Informal concerts where anyone, staff or pupils, can show up and play whatever they want to were loved in one school where I worked. St Andrew's Day in another school was a chance for past and present pupils to celebrate the life of the school across the ages, so to speak. Alumni and former teachers would write in to the school, wishing pupils and staff well. All the letters or emails would be posted on a board for all to see. Some schools make much of giving colours (a tie or a badge or a certificate) to mark special achievement, usually in a sport but more recently also given for drama or art or citizenship or whatever else the school holds to be important. We thrive on symbols and they can do much to draw communities together. Look up on YouTube (youtu.be/M6Qtc_zlGhcthe) the Haka tribute given by the school's pupils out of respect for the life of their teacher, Mr Dawson Tamatea, as the hearse arrives for his funeral. If you are left dry-eyed, you are a heartless individual.

Teachers love to create their own rituals in their classes. I certainly did. A two-second applause for an individual who had done something small, but notable, did so much to make pupils feel good about themselves. When I was a head, I used to love, at the end-of-term prize-giving, surprising the staff by handing out one or two prizes to *them*, and not just to the children. It was usually just to recognise something out of the ordinary. The kids would whoop and cheer for the unsuspecting member of staff as they came up to receive a certificate. The teacher felt great. There are so many ways we can celebrate achievement, have fun together, show respect and demonstrate oneness. School is the perfect place to develop all of this.

Just remember, the night before school starts really doesn't have to be awful.

Gerald Roberts – creator of intrigue

As a secondary school pupil, I was even more lacking in confidence than the average diffident teenager in my year. I would so hate to be a 14-year-old again: you can't walk down a corridor without wondering what the pictures on the wall might be thinking of you. Everyone is (obviously) looking at you the entire time. Spots and teeth braces mean you are simply not fit to be seen. Your body is doing weird things. You're permanently tired. Everyone has expectations of you (you got it right, Charles Dickens). You're the hairy caterpillar, the ugly duckling, the useless tadpole in life's cruel cycle.

The model of calm at such a turbulent time in my life was a teacher who knew how to make things easier for us. Gerald Roberts taught me English in my first year and again for A level. He was my head of year in the run up to exams at the age of 16. He always gave me the impression that he liked me and enjoyed talking to me. Even though I could hardly string two sentences together coherently at the time, he made me think I had something of value to say. He let me have a desk in the coveted space of the 'long room', where I could get on with my work in peace. He spotted that I was quite a good organiser and signed me up for running various competitions and tournaments. When I got into a bit of trouble and was influenced rather too heavily by another pupil with some quite obnoxious views on life, he gently questioned me so as to get me to reflect on what was happening. He got me back on track without it ever seeming like a big deal. He didn't have to do this, of course. But he was determined to help me, at such an impressionable age. The conceit in my title, *Mining for Gold*, denotes an arduous task, not just a magical one. Gerry went the extra mile for me and I'd like to think, discovered something precious in my potential.

Gerry, as we all called him (not to his face, obvs), was intriguing.

We could never quite work out what he was thinking. He was the kind of teacher who was quite happy to allow silences in the lesson. He'd ask a question and just wait until someone answered. He was intensely interested in us and his subject. He saw humour wherever he looked. Somehow we seemed to fascinate him. We were in awe of his intellect. You'd walk into his study and he'd have Berlioz playing on his sound system while marking a pile of essays. On top of reading all the books he was teaching to his classes, he'd constantly be working his way through other huge tomes, such as *Moby Dick*, none less than about 600 pages. He was deeply interested in the life of the mind. He found Chaucer intriguing and delightful. He wanted to take us on a journey of discovery. We'd be quiet in the middle of a lesson as he stumbled on a passage where he thought a jewel was hiding, and we'd all wait as he absorbed himself for what felt like ages. He'd make funny noises to himself, which we found intriguing of course.

He always remembered to set us homework and he always marked it on time. We never doubted that he would deliver. His lessons were meticulously planned in an exercise book, yet he was quite prepared to go off script or wander left field. I remember him inviting us, as 13-year-olds, to act out a poem by Dylan Thomas or some other Welsh poet and staying completely nonchalant as we (naturally) wove football hooliganism, shouting and swearing and general debauchery into our interpretations. He was encouraging, praising the odd bit that might have had any merit whatsoever, and making us think that we had worked well. In doing so, he got us to enjoy the subject and feel that we could engage well with the material. He laid down a platform of confidence amongst us, so that a surprisingly large portion of the class ended up taking English at A level, when we knew he would be one of our main teachers.

I think Gerry, more than most teachers, made me realise that teaching could be a rich intellectual pursuit as you sought to understand your pupils and the way they interacted with your subject. He knew that we had no natural inclination to study Chaucer's *Canterbury Tales*, but found a way to draw us in to what was, after all, a medieval romp, full of sex and foul play to match anything on television today. He knew how to read the text as it would have been spoken originally, or at least he made us believe that his reading was authentic. We loved to watch his face come alive as he clearly so enjoyed the experience. You could almost see/hear the bizarre group of nuns and priests and other people talking to each other on their pilgrimage.

I remember the last school report he wrote. The words, 'He might get a B' screamed from the page. A 'B' in those days was enough to get you into law or medicine. A cousin of mine was accepted for medicine on BCD. Only the most outstanding performances got As. So, getting a B was a mark of real achievement and meant that I was up there with the rest of the class. I still remember the feeling of elation I had from reading that one sentence.

Reports were different then. Teachers didn't feel under any obligation to soften their comments. One of my favourites from my own school reports came from my French teacher when I was 10 or 11:

He has a voice like a siren, but generally, at least, it is a warning that something correct is coming your way.

Ho ho. They don't make 'em like that anymore. Gerry's reports were always acutely succinct and every word was measured. Because I respected him so much, I gave so much more value to his, than to those of other teachers.

I am grateful to him, even now, for believing in me and getting me to the point where I could achieve such a respectable grade. I did in fact get a B, but of course am frustrated even now that I didn't manage an A. I know that if only I'd spent a bit more time revising the modern British novel paper texts, I could have done it. Not that I still give it much thought, you understand.

So...

Teaching is fascinating, difficult, endlessly demanding, inspiring, full of comic moments. Most of all, though, it is a hugely significant role in our society. You don't need to mould yourself into some ideal. Just be you, because even little you, with the odd quirks, can be a brilliant teacher. You can be effective, in your own way.

To do that, of course, you have to find out what works, but it is quite likely that someone else has already overcome the problem you are facing. So, go and watch other teachers. You will find it fascinating. Invite them back, of course.

Don't be scared to develop your own idiosyncrasies and, well, eccentricities. Most of the effective teachers in this book, including myself, have enjoyed being a bit different. Fortunately, this is a job that encourages personality. Enjoy.

Remember, it's your kingdom. You rule. Teach them to be the kind of citizens you want them to be. In doing so, you are modelling how you want them to be for the rest of their lives.

But it is a tough role. Children, well, people, are complex. A huge journey of discovery on your part is required, where flexibility should be second nature to you.

Do not accept, ever, that your pupils can't succeed. Destroy any negativity they have developed about your subject, or you. Getting a young person to believe they can perform is one of the greatest gifts you will give to them.

Be ruthlessly encouraging.

Make a note of your impact. Others won't tell you enough. Keep a list of your students and follow up what happens to them when they leave you.

Don't burn out. Work a sensible day, where you build in enjoyment and relaxation. It is your impact that matters, not your effort. But hard work helps, of course.

Don't let your talent wilt. Feed it, nurture it. Study, read, reflect, discuss, watch. You're a professional: this is your responsibility.

To system leaders, I challenge you to pay teachers well. Or, at least, pay them to the extent that they don't worry about what they are being paid. We are not so naive as to think that pay is the principal way in which we will get people to join the profession or keep them. Teachers, more than anything, need to be encouraged by the impact they are making. That's the task of school leaders. School governing bodies, or multi-academy trust boards, should encourage tracking the progress of past pupils to celebrate their achievements. Most independent schools have been doing this for decades. Looking after alumni is not (just) a way of attracting additional funding to the school; it also demonstrates the long-lasting impact of the teaching they received when they were with the school and the way these people were shaped for life by the culture of the school. There should be a significant motivating impact on the teachers, who should be hugely proud of what they have achieved. Some schools produce an inordinate number of doctors or netball internationals or whatever. Why? It's not the school *per se*, but the teachers of those subjects who have influenced, encouraged, hassled (think of Mo Farah) or whatever.

A brilliant teacher can spot wrong thinking and correct it. That is highly skilful, and extraordinarily difficult to do. Gerry Roberts did it for me. It's part of the moral tutor role of teaching. You have a task to help *form* individuals.

Your talent needs developing over time, so stick around.

Remember that your role as a teacher is mining for gold in every person you work with. Find it, and you release value in that individual that lasts for life.

Do please pass on any comments or questions by writing to me at fergal. roche@thekeysupport.com.

Acknowledgements

I have been dead lucky. Not only have I worked in a number of different schools, but my job has afforded me the chance to visit well over a hundred schools all over the country. I normally go with a colleague and we sit down with the head and maybe another member of the senior team. We grill them for a couple of hours all about their school, what they have done, why some things have worked and others haven't. Because they know I've been a teacher and a head myself, they are quite forgiving when I ask really chancy questions, like 'who's your best teacher and why?' Or, 'If you can't manage to recruit teachers round here, what are you going to do then?' They usually give us a tour. At the end I pretty much always apologise for being so hard and for taking so much time, but usually they thank us for an excellent use of two hours. Strange. Anyway, if you've been one of those school leaders, thank you for your patience.

I love talking to teachers about what they are doing. I have quite a kinship with them and they make me feel more normal when I see quite how eccentric some of them are. To the several hundred who have given me access to their classrooms, thank you.

I'd like to thank in particular the teachers at St Gabriel's College in Brixton and the seven schools in the GEP Academies Trust in and around Guildford. I walked through tough times with the St Gabriel's guys and saw their belief and hard work pay off: I am in awe. I love what you have managed to achieve with such a diverse range of children. I am just getting used to GEP and am excited with what you want to achieve, but am thrilled with the vision you have developed for children across the area.

There aren't many teachers in my family. I hope there will be more (hint hint, kids). But whenever I go over to West Cork where lots of relations live, the respect that Bantry people have for my teacher aunt, Deidre, and uncle Matt (who ran the technical college) Kingston is huge. They have clearly had a lasting impact on that town and they both inspired me over the years.

Just as I was finishing the book, my great friend of 35 years who was with me in the Jesuits, died, after an illness lasting less than three months. Mario D'Souza was only 61. He was a Catholic priest and a professor of the Philosophy of Education at the University of St Michael's College in the University of Toronto. He had a significant impact on my thinking over the years. I was hoping to delight him with the news that I had given him a mention, but it was too late. He meant a lot to me.

Colleagues at The Key inspire me on a daily basis. I have never before worked with such a talented group of people who want to change the world through their work. Every day they send round on email or Slack the feedback from schools that are thanking us for some little thing that we have done for them. In doing so, staff show the pride they have in the work we do as a company. Thank you guys. At this point, they would usually expect a 'smiley Fergal', an emoticon of a horrible picture of me smiling. I've got used to it.

I'd never have written this book if Alex Sharratt from John Catt hadn't kept hassling me. Because he always did so in the nicest way possible, I eventually gave in. Originally I told him I had an idea for a Christmas book, but he gently persuaded me that I could manage more. The thought of writing a *whole* book was highly intimidating so I asked Ewa Josefkowicz, one of my colleagues who has written a couple of children's novels that are soon to be published, what the shortest acceptable book length would be. 35-40,000 words, she said, with authority. I decided that, if I were ever to read a book like this, myself, I'd only want to read a few pages at a time. So I got a big piece of A3 card and drew a grid to give me 30 boxes. Then I spent a couple of weeks thinking through the teachers and lecturers I really wanted to mention and slotted them in. Originally I had told Alex that he should get an education expert to write the intervening chapters, but there were a few points I wanted to make, so I came up with some ideas myself, and before I knew it, I'd filled the empty boxes. How we surprise ourselves.

Writing the thing was really not too painful at all. A few years ago, the cricketer Jonathan Trott scored over 200 runs in a test match, batting for many hours. Interviewed afterwards, he was asked how he possibly managed to keep going. 'I only thought about the next five runs,' he said.

So, I wondered whether I could write five chapters. When I had done so, I thought about getting to ten, which would be a third of the way through. When I got to 15, I wrote back to Alex and told him I could do the whole thing myself and would finish within three months. He kept encouraging me to the extent that I went mad one long weekend and finished the whole thing a month ahead of schedule. So, if you're thinking you could never write a book: been there, thought that, you're wrong. *If I can, you really, really can.*

Thank you to all the people who reviewed the book. Two people said they would, but never came back to us. Either you thought it was rubbish or you've failed to hand your work in on time. If the latter, remember: your names are on our list and a detention awaits...